Understanding
COM+

The Architecture for Enterprise Development
Using Microsoft® Technologies

David S. Platt
Foreword by Greg Hope,
Lead Architect, COM+

PUBLISHED BY
Microsoft Press
A Division of Microsoft Corporation
One Microsoft Way
Redmond, Washington 98052-6399

Copyright © 1999 by David S. Platt

Library of Congress Cataloging-in-Publication Data pending.

Printed and bound in the United States of America.

3 4 5 6 7 8 9   WCWC   4 3 2 1 0

Distributed in Canada by Penguin Books Canada Limited.

A CIP catalogue record for this book is available from the British Library.

Microsoft Press books are available through booksellers and distributors worldwide. For further
information about international editions, contact your local Microsoft Corporation office or contact
Microsoft Press International directly at fax (425) 936-7329. Visit our Web site at mspress.microsoft.com.

Acquisitions Editor: Ben Ryan
Project Editor: Mary Kalbach Barnard
Technical Editor: Jack Beaudry

To my wife, Linda

Contents

Chapter Six

In-Memory Database 185

Chapter Seven

Load Balancing 207

Foreword

COM is a silent, enabling technology. It is pure plumbing, boring and inert, without a component-based tool or application to bring it to life and implement a useful solution. My personal test of a great COM-based tool or application is that the developer, user, and administrator have never heard of COM. As a result of this stealthy nature, it is often surprising to people just how many applications have COM inside them.

In 1992, Tony Williams and Bob Atkinson (the original architects of COM) defined a simple jewel that time after time various groups inside and outside Microsoft have used to address a wide variety of problem domains. Compound documents or object linking and embedding? COM. Scripting and automation? COM. ActiveX controls and Authenticode? COM. Universal Data Access? COM. Microsoft Transaction Server and Microsoft Distributed Transaction Coordinator? COM. Microsoft SNA Server Transaction Integrator? COM. Get the picture?

COM's flexibility in addressing this wide variety of requirements in a consistent way has clearly established its position as the world's most successful object model. The debate about whether object-oriented programming and component software design is a good idea is finally over. COM provides a simple and uniform model for component-based development that has been proven in practice. Today 3 million developers employ a broad set of COM tools to build the COM applications used by over 200 million Windows users daily.

It is worthwhile to step back and briefly examine what we are trying to enable here and what COM's role is in the bigger picture. In his latest book, *Business @ the Speed of Thought* (Warner Books, 1999), Bill Gates addresses the following to CEOs: "Business is going to change more in the next ten years than it has in the last fifty" and "How you gather, manage, and use information will determine whether you win or lose." He then describes a step-by-step program for implementing a digital nervous system to enable information flow, and discusses the role of Microsoft Windows DNA as the application architecture. Pretty heady stuff. And, you ask, what exactly binds Windows DNA together? You guessed it. COM.

Based on where we are right now, COM+ 1.0 represents a significant, yet incremental and additive advance in COM. COM+ 1.0 is specifically designed to leverage and enhance prior investments in COM, MTS, and other COM-based applications. Digging deeper, the "plus" in COM+ 1.0 revolves around three fundamental design centers.

First, it is both a better COM and a better MTS due to deep integration of these two previously separate technologies. The concepts of context, class attributes, and interception are so deeply imbedded that powerful services are cleanly and independently implemented. Services mesh more seamlessly, with improved performance and reliability. Some previously problematic scenarios—such as abnormal teminations while debugging—now simply work.

Second, existing services such as transactions, security, administration, and surrogates are not only better because of this superior interception architecture, but their specific features are richer and enhanced in both depth and breadth. I won't attempt to list these features here; suffice it to say that COM applications already utilizing these services have suddenly become a lot more powerful and flexible.

Finally, there are fundamental new services, such as Queued Components for disconnected messaging, the Event service for loosely coupled publish-and-subscribe events, In-Memory Database (IMDB) for high-speed transactionally consistent data caching, and component load balancing and object pooling for building scalable application clusters. We hope these "new and improved" services make it easier to develop, deploy, and use COM+ applications.

Looking forward, we see no finish line. While there is encouraging evidence that we are heading in the right direction, we have much work ahead of us. COM+ and related technologies must continue to evolve to meet changing market requirements. Significant factors include the continued transition from desktop and client-server to N-Tier Web Computing, as well as the simplicity, reliability, and form factors required for Appliance Computing. Stay tuned.

In this book, Dave Platt walks you through COM+ 1.0, using a friendly and refreshingly consistent top-down approach to purpose, concept, and code. Dave has drawn extensively on his "roll your own" experiences and offers numerous anecdotes about the shortcomings of this approach, motivating his "Let go and let COM+" advice. Dave has researched COM+ carefully, both on his own and with the support of the COM+ product team. This book is a must-read for managers and developers who want to understand and implement a great application with COM+ as their silent partner.

Greg Hope
Architect
Microsoft COM+ Team

Acknowledgments

Everything in life is connected. Where do you start thanking people who contributed to any given slice—for example, helping me with this book? With Ben Ryan, the Microsoft Press acquisitions editor I met at WinDev West last fall, who recruited me? With Jeff Prosise, who organized the sushi outing where I met Ben? With Kim Crouse, who snagged me for WinDev three years previously? With whoever mentioned my name to her in the first place? With Mrs. Johnson, the high-school English teacher who taught me that a precise verb was worth a dozen adjectives? With my great grand-father Shmuel Platovsky, who emigrated from Russia in 1895?

I'll start with the team at Microsoft Press. Ben Ryan got the ball rolling. I initially proposed a code-based book, similar to my first three. He liked that idea at first, but then came back and said, "Hey, how about a high-level conceptual book on COM+, sort of like David Chappell's book on ActiveX?" The next acknowledgment has to go to Mary Barnard, my project editor on this book. I had never worked on a book project with a real editor before. I did my previous books on my own, with a little help from non-technical proofreaders who thought my C++ examples contained too many semicolons. I was really worried that working through an editor would stifle my voice (which, love it or hate it, you will have to agree is distinctive). That's not what happened. I thought my prose was pretty good, at least for a geek. I nearly hit the ceiling when I saw how many edits she had made in the first draft, until I started reading them. Then I started saying to myself, "Wait a minute, that's exactly what I wanted to say, only better." Sometimes it took us a couple of go-rounds to get the phrasing right. I've come to the conclusion the writing is better with an editor, at least the right one. I could spend my time thinking about the best analogy to explain a particular technical point, instead of subject-verb agreement. And if I felt strongly about any point, she'd let it through. (There's one exception in the entire book: I wanted a trademark symbol on a couple of application names that aren't really trademarks, but should be; I'll let you guess what they are. I think I now understand the phrase "freedom of my chains.") Jack Beaudry did a great job as technical editor, testing sample applications and answering questions like "How do you capitalize ProgID?" John Pierce, managing editor, read the book behind Mary and supplied the clout to keep it the way it is. Hats off to the comp, art, and proofreading folks. Thanks to all of you for making it a much better product than I could have done on my own. We make a good team, and I'd be happy to do it again.

It's one thing to be able to write, it's another to know something to write about. COM+ would have long gone obsolete if I'd had to figure it out on my own before writing about it. The main reason that I switched to Microsoft Press from my previous publisher was the opportunity to sit down with the programmers who were actually making COM+ happen and hear their story. I couldn't buy that at any price. Everyone on the COM+ team at Microsoft was really superb; even in the face of their killer schedules, they took the time to explain the details of COM+ to me, often several times, until I got it right. First honors here have to go to Mary Kirtland. She knew the answers to many of my questions and tracked down the ones she didn't. She set up a mind-crushing two-day marathon at Microsoft that had me lurching from one geek to another, trying to retain everything I was learning about COM+. She got me the prerelease versions of the software I needed to perform tests and take screen shots. Greg Hope set the stage with his explanation of context and what it means to be an object in the COM+ environment. His statement that "COM will be successful when no one knows that he is using it," sticks with me today. Dick Dievendorff and George Chung hung in there with me until I got the gestalt of Queued Components. Joe Long and Scott Robinson explained the nuts and bolts of context, Steve Jamieson the Compensating Resource Manager, and Joyce Etheridge some of the ins and outs of interacting with other transactioning systems. Markus Horstmann explained the catalog and administrative features of COM+ (and why the term *application* was chosen over *package*). Shawn Woods explained the newly revised Event service, and Senthil Kumar Natarajan supplied some critical sample code and the answers to make it work, with help from Don McCrady and Radu Palanca. Marc Levy showed me around the COM+ security system with such adeptness that I hope he never turns crooked. Amit Mital explained COM+ load balancing. Henry Lau and Jocelyn Garner explained the In-Memory Database, and my research assistant Paul Holley did valuable background work on that chapter. Richard Ersek, Chris Whitaker, Robert Barnes, Tarun Anand, Emily Kruglick, Phil Garrett, and Wolfgang Manousek helped Mary Kirtland track down answers to some of my questions.

Above all, I have to thank my wife, Linda. Without her unflagging support, I'd never be able to write a book or do much of anything else.

David S. Platt
www.rollthunder.com
Ipswich, Massachusetts
May 1999

Chapter One

COM Plus What?

Enterprise—The Final Frontier

Personal computers have reached the point where essentially anything an individual might want to do on his own is automated for
him. Track contacts? Done. Write a pointless memo? Piece of
cake, with style sheets and wizards to make sure no smidgen of
sense creeps in inadvertently. Play Solitaire? OK, new variations
keep evolving, but you get my point. Nobody develops word processors anymore because they've been done. The fact that very
few new features have been added to the Microsoft Foundation
Classes for the last two years should underscore the point that the
desktop has matured, that there are relatively few new features to
add to it. Where is the next frontier in which the PC software mar-
ketplace will continue its stunning growth?

Remember how Microsoft Windows versions 1 and 2 flailed
around irrelevantly for about five years? Microsoft practically gave
them away in Cracker Jack boxes, and still no one would use
them because they didn't offer enough useful, convenient, time-
saving features. Windows didn't take off until enough users had
386 PCs on their desks, mostly wasting the capability of that chip
by using it as a souped-up AT. Windows 3.x took advantage of the
critical mass of this unmined resource to produce a pretty good
MS-DOS multitasker that also played Solitaire, and the rest is history. The entire modern PC environment dates from that moment.

The desktop computer
has matured—there are
relatively few new
features to add to it.

Even though most PCs today are tied into a network of some sort, they don't usually interact with each other at an application level.

A similar revolution is now taking place in the computing world. The Internet has mushroomed to the point where nearly every PC in the world is connected to it at some time for some purpose—a simple modem for occasional informational e-mail, a dedicated high-speed line for downloading pornographic movies. However, even though most PCs today are tied into a network of some sort, they don't usually interact with each other at an application level. They use the network for sending human-readable e-mail, sharing a printer, maybe a hard disk. PCs are still islands connected by messages in bottles, albeit unusually fast ones.

The next frontier of application development is the distributed system, otherwise known as the enterprise system, where different programs on different machines actually interact with each other. Application developers are only now beginning to plow this fallow field. And COM+ is the seed.

The classic definition of an enterprise application comprises three main points—it is large, it is distributed, and it is mission critical.

The classic definition of an enterprise application comprises three main points—an enterprise application is large, it is distributed, and it is mission critical. For this book I will insist only on the first two points: an enterprise application is large, at least compared to a single desktop application, and it is distributed—it runs on more than one computer at a time. Enterprise applications used to be mission critical because they cost so much that no one could afford to write one unless their business couldn't operate without it—for example, an airline reservation system. However, this situation is changing even as I write these words and you read them. The prefabricated enterprise application infrastructure provided by COM+ makes enterprise applications much easier to write and therefore much less expensive than ever before, so I expect to see many more of them, quite soon. I consider a large, distributed multiplayer role-playing game and a large, distributed application that controls North American air defense to both be enterprise applications, even though the latter is mission critical and the former isn't (unless you have a lot of money riding on the championship). Again, for the purposes of this book, an enterprise application is simply large and distributed.

Enterprise Development Challenges

Enterprise applications are not new. Programmers in large organizations such as banks, airlines, insurance companies, and hospitals have been struggling with them for years. Developing enterprise applications has historically been a very long, very painful, very expensive, and frequently not very successful task. It's not that an application's business logic was hideously complex; the main stumbling block was that a developer had to write from scratch all the infrastructure needed to scale that business logic up to the enterprise level. For example, an enterprise application requires a high degree of security, which is unnecessary for a desktop application. The developers of an enterprise application have to write (and test, and debug, and deploy, and support, and maintain, while employees come and go) all the code for the security system—how it authenticates users, how it decides whether a user is or is not allowed to do this or that, the tools administrators use to set or remove users' security permissions. Enterprise applications contain many other infrastructural challenges, such as pooling resources, serializing access to shared resources, synchronizing atomic transactions over multiple servers and databases, and deploying applications to multiple client machines. Writing this infrastructure takes time, costs lots of money (with relatively low unit volume to amortize it over), and the code is damnably difficult to debug and verify.

Developing enterprise applications has traditionally been a very long, very painful, very expensive, and frequently not very successful task.

This enterprise infrastructure has nothing whatsoever to do with banking or medicine or airline reservations or whatever it is that an enterprise application needs to do. But one enterprise application's infrastructure is very similar to another's—the user identification system of a banking application is very much like that of a medical application, the thread resource pooler of an

One enterprise application's infrastructure is very similar to another's.

airline reservation application is identical to that of a supermarket application, and so on. Wouldn't it be cool if someone wrote all that enterprise infrastructure just once? Wrote it so you could inherit[1] the pieces you cared about and spend your time writing your own business logic? And then integrated this infrastructure into the operating system you're already paying for? COM+ provides this solution.

What the Heck Is COM+ Anyway?

COM+ is an advanced COM run-time environment that provides prefabricated solutions to many of the generic infrastructural problems faced by enterprise application designers, particularly the infrastructural problems of the middle, business tier in the three-tier model. If you think of the product as "Microsoft Enterprise Application Prefabricated Functionality Toolkit," you'll have the right mental model.

COM+ is an integrated part of Windows 2000. It would be premature to say anything in print about a shipping schedule for Windows 2000, but there's a good chance it will be after this book appears on bookstore shelves.

COM+ provides two significant enhancements to COM. First, it is version 3 of Microsoft Transaction Server (MTS), updated and integrated into the existing portions of COM to provide a seamless whole. MTS, which first shipped in the spring of 1997, was Microsoft's first attempt to provide any type of enterprise infrastructure as a product. As will be discussed in Chapter 2, MTS used to be a separate wrapper layer that sat on top of COM. The MTS and COM groups at Microsoft were merged in the fall of 1997, and this is their first integrated product. COM+ enhances and upgrades the following MTS services:

COM+ is an advanced COM run-time environment that provides prefabricated solutions to many of the generic infrastructural problems faced by enterprise application designers.

COM+ is version 3 of Microsoft Transaction Server, updated and integrated into the existing portions of COM to provide a seamless whole.

---

1. The word *inherit* strikes a deep emotional chord in object oriented programmers. In this book, I am using it in its most generic sense, of something valuable dumped in your lap in return for no effort on your part, something you probably don't deserve and will likely squander. I'm not using it in the narrow OO sense of the word.

- *Transaction Services* Transactions are a mechanism for ensuring data integrity in a distributed system, even in the face of communication or machine failure. The transaction services of COM+ provide an easy way for COM objects to create, use, and vote on the outcomes of transactions. These services are described in Chapter 3.

- *Security Services* Essentially all enterprise applications care about security. They need to make sure that only authorized users are allowed to perform important operations. Writing security code using the raw Windows NT security mechanism was and continues to be a nightmare. COM+'s security services provide an easy way to specify security administratively, without writing any code at all. These services also provide a much easier way to write programmatic security logic for situations too complex for the administrative mechanism to handle. Security services are described in Chapter 2.

- *Synchronization Services* Architects of distributed systems need to protect certain critical portions of their components against the possibility of concurrent access by multiple threads. Writing code to do this takes a long time, costs a lot of money, and is extremely difficult to get right. The synchronization services of COM+ provide an easy way to specify a component's synchronization requirements administratively without the need for code. These services also provide an easier way to write programmatic synchronization logic for situations too complex for the administrative mechanism to handle. Chapter 2 discusses these synchronization services.

Second, COM+ includes four new run-time services, specified as follows, that make it easier to solve the problems unique to enterprise applications:

COM+ includes four new run-time services that make it easier to solve the problems unique to enterprise applications.

- *Queued Components* This is a communication mechanism that allows COM clients to make calls on a COM object when the object's server machine is not reachable on the network—for example, during disconnected operation. The calls are recorded by a system utility, transmitted to the server through asynchronous protocols, and played back by another system utility into the server-side COM object when the server machine becomes available. This mechanism makes it much easier to write enterprise applications because neither client nor server needs to care about the other's lifetime. Think of queued components as e-mail or a phone-answering machine for COM calls. The Queued Components mechanism is described in Chapter 4.

- *Event Service*   A publisher is any program in an enterprise application that provides information updates, such as changes in stock prices. A subscriber is likewise any program in an enterprise application that receives these notifications. The Event service of COM+ provides an easy way for subscribers to sign up to receive these notifications from publishers, and for publishers to locate and make calls to their subscribers. Chapter 5 provides a discussion of this service.

- *In-Memory Database*   IMDB is a service that provides automatic memory caching of back-end tables on middle-tier machines. It can enormously speed up access to database tables that are primarily read from rather than written to, such as those for mail-order catalogs. COM+'s IMDB service is described in Chapter 6.

- *Load Balancing*   The client load on an enterprise application frequently causes it to outgrow a single server. COM+'s load-balancing service provides an automatic mechanism for distributing object creation requests among a number of servers in a pool, thereby spreading the load. This service is discussed in Chapter 7.

COM+ is not a radical shift in world view.

That's what COM+ is; how about what it isn't? First, it is not the radical shift in worldview that was demanded by the transition from MS-DOS to Windows, or by COM when it first appeared.

You still write COM classes using standard development environments such as Visual Basic or Visual C++; the difference is that the classes get more brains from the operating system than they used to, making them faster and easier to write. Clients still create COM objects using the *CreateObject* or *CoCreateInstance* functions; there's just more prefabricated functionality between the function and the object, again provided by the operating system. Yes, there is a shift in the worldview, but it's more subtle.

In one sense, COM+ is really just the Windows 2000 release of COM, with incrementally more new features to solve new problems. The number of new features is just larger than before, and a case can be made for cooler as well. Simply calling it COM would not differentiate between this version and earlier ones, and I feel that the distinction is necessary. I could call it the W2KVoC, but that would take too long to write and be impossible to pronounce, although making up acronyms for this release of COM might amuse some frustrated geek with nothing better to do on a lonely Saturday night. It could be worse; Microsoft could have called it Active Services, or some other longer and vaguer marketing buzzword. At least COM+ only takes one more character, and I'm already holding the shift key down when I type "COM."

In a sense, COM+ is really just the Windows 2000 release of COM, with incrementally more new features to solve new problems.

This release of COM+ is not what Mary Kirtland wrote about in the November and December 1997 issues of *Microsoft Systems Journal*. As she said later in the notes for the Fall 1998 PDC, "Those articles are out of date…Forget everything I said last year about COM+." As Ron Ziegler, Richard Nixon's press secretary during Watergate, said, "Yesterday's statement is now inoperative." The articles were based on some very early prototype work, and as often happens in turning a prototype into a product, plans changed. I think you should take those articles philosophically, like, "Hey, these are some interesting ideas we've been kicking around. Wouldn't it be nice if someday…" No one at Microsoft is commenting on future versions today, but yes, it would be nice, wouldn't it?

My First Enterprise System

Here's an example of what can happen when you try to write an enterprise system without prefabricated infrastructure.

Here's a real-life example of an attempt to write an enterprise system without prefabricated infrastructure. It was the first one I worked on, about 15 years ago, a foreign exchange trading application for use by major banks. At the time, traders in a bank's foreign exchange room had to fill out paper deal tickets with a pencil each time they made a deal. These tickets were collected at the end of the day and the information was entered manually into the bank's central computer. This approach had a number of problems, however. In the heat of battle, the traders understandably did not want to stop making deals to take the time to fill out a deal ticket. The tickets would be lost, be filled out illegibly, be transcribed incorrectly. The paper ticket support staff was large, expensive, and needed extensive training. And even when the paper ticket worked perfectly, it didn't provide any information for analysts until the beginning of the next day. A trader couldn't tell at any given moment during the trading day whether she was long or short in sterling or marks. A trader with better information could clean her clock, and often did.

The system I worked on was to replace the paper deal tickets with direct electronic entry. Each trader would have a PC and enter information about a deal by using a touch screen. The PC would talk to a server, another PC, where the deals would be recorded. The dealer's user interface would provide a convenient rate calculator so the traders would actually use it. All data entry would be done with a keyboard or touch screen, so the traders' handwriting didn't come into play, although keying errors could certainly still happen. Transcription and entry would be eliminated both as a source of errors and as a cost center. Position data would be available in real time. The system could conceivably interface with other trading equipment, automatically entering a trader's counterparty based on the phone connection in current use. Similar functionality was available on systems costing $50K or more per workstation. We tried to do it on 286 MS-DOS boxes, to sell for about $10K per seat, with ongoing support and training revenues.

It didn't work. We didn't understand the unique problems of writing enterprise software—at least I didn't, and if any of the other programmers or managers did, they disguised it very well. We all had single desktop PC mindsets. An airline pilot once told me that every warning label in the cockpit was written in blood. Every lesson we learned about enterprise infrastructure was written in sweat, tears, and agony.

Every lesson we learned about enterprise infrastructure was written in sweat, tears, and agony.

For example, the servers sent out periodic updates of exchange rates on the system network, but the network didn't offer reliable delivery. Every once in a while one workstation would miss an update and display the wrong rate until it was overwritten by the next update. Updates usually happened too quickly for the lost one to matter, but once in a while the lost update applied to a price that seldom changed and the trader would notice. Since the same rates were coming in from other sources, the wrong rate would stand out and would usually be noticed before anyone lost any money, but the trader would go ballistic. We had to write a sequencing mechanism to detect lost packets, which we completed, and then a refresh mechanism to update all the rates, which we never got done. The Event service of COM+ could have handled this for us with ease.

For another example, a system of this type obviously requires security. Only authorized traders are allowed to enter deals. Some traders are only allowed to deal in certain currencies, others only with certain counterparties, and so on. We had to write all of our own security code to enforce all of these restrictions. You just can't afford to do this. To be effective, the security programming team has to be smarter than the smartest crook. You need a dedicated team that does nothing but eat, sleep, and drink security for years, because that's what the opposition has. We didn't have a team like this and couldn't afford one. For example, we encrypted all passwords transmitted on the network, but the encrypted password was the same every time. To break into the system, a thief would only have to record the packet (which I later did as a

You can't afford to write all the security code demanded by an enterprise system.

demonstration) and play it back. The security mechanisms of COM+ are the product of a very sharp group at Microsoft who devote their lives to security code. You'd better hope none of them turn crooked.

The transaction infrastructure provided by COM+ solves the problem of database integrity.

For yet another example, we didn't have any mechanism for ensuring database integrity. Every once in a while, the server machine that held the deal database would fall over dead. MS-DOS did that, especially when you pushed the envelope on it. The problem was that if the server went down while it was in the middle of storing a deal in the database, there was no good automatic way of recovering from the failure. A skilled operator had to use Norton Utilities to examine the deal file and manually reconstruct the failed record. It didn't happen often, but when it did, many people were quite unhappy. The transaction infrastructure provided by COM+ would have solved this problem neatly.

COM+ enables you to inherit infrastructure from the operating system.

What killed us (apart from a crooked boss who canceled the programmers' health insurance without telling anyone) was having to take the time and spend the money to write infrastructure code. We couldn't buy it—at that time nobody sold it, at least not for a PC environment. If we were developing this software today, we would simply inherit this infrastructure from the operating system. It wasn't the business logic that did us in: Calculating foreign exchange cross rates isn't all that hard. Figuring out which days are holidays in different countries to calculate a settlement date is tedious, but not that difficult. I occasionally wonder how long it would take to put together this kind of system today. A whole lot less time than it took us to NOT do it, so many years ago.

About This Book

My previous books were essentially low-level how-to manuals and tutorials, where I spent most of my time discussing listings of program code. This approach worked beautifully for geeks who program in C++. Unfortunately, this was a small percentage of the people who buy computer books, which made my creditors very unhappy. As applications are being split into several tiers, so the developer population is segmenting among the different languages for the different tiers—Microsoft Visual Basic or HTML for the presentation tier, often Microsoft Visual C++ or Microsoft Visual J++ for the middle tier, database languages for the data tier. I wanted this book to be accessible to developers who weren't comfortable in Visual C++, or for whom C++ didn't match their problem domains. Furthermore, I found that managers got essentially nothing out of my C++ based approach because they never worked the sample programs (with only one exception I know of, and I'm sending him a free copy of this book for working so hard to understand my last one). And an ignorant (or worse, half-educated) manager is an extremely dangerous beast. Give me a wounded tiger any day.

To make this book more accessible to more people, I adopted the writing format that David Chappell used so successfully in his book *Understanding ActiveX and OLE* (Microsoft Press, 1996): lots of explanations, lots of diagrams, and very little code in the text descriptions. But much as I liked that book, I still felt hungry for code (as I often need a piece of chocolate cake to top off a meal of delicate sushi). I found myself writing code to help me understand his ideas, much as I wrote equations to understand the textual descriptions in Stephen Hawking's *A Brief History of Time* (OK, I'm a geek). So my book comes with sample programs for all the chapters, some of which I wrote myself and some of which I adopted from the Microsoft Platform SDK. These programs are available on this book's Web site, *http://mspress.microsoft.com/mspress/products/3282/*, which will also provide installation instructions and pointers to other relevant sites. Managers will be able to read the book without drowning in code, while code-hungry geeks will still be able to slake their appetites.

> Sample programs, installation instructions, and pointers to other relevant sites are available on this book's Web site.

Each chapter presents a single topic from the top down. I start off by describing the business problem that needs to be solved. I then explain the high-level architecture of the infrastructure that COM+ provides to help you solve that problem while writing a minimum of code. I next walk you through the simplest example I

> Each chapter presents a single topic from the top down.

can find that employs the solution. Managers may want to stop reading after this section. I then continue with a discussion of finer points—other possibilities, boundary cases, and the like. Throughout, I've tried to follow Pournelle's Law, coined by Jerry Pournelle in his "Chaos Manor" computing column in the original *Byte* magazine (now resurrected on the Web at *http://www.byte.com*, and featuring yours truly as the new ActiveX/COM columnist), which states simply, "You can never have too many examples."

Warning: Prerelease Software

The fundamental trade-off of writing a book on cutting-edge software is accuracy vs. timeliness.

Contemporary software is the fastest-changing field of human thought that has ever existed. The fundamental trade-off of writing a book on cutting-edge software is accuracy vs. timeliness. If you wait to start writing until the software actually ships, the book appears on shelves six months to a year after the software does. That's often half the lifetime of the product or more. On the other hand, if you start writing too early in the development process, the final release of the software often bears little resemblance to what the book describes. I've always tried to delay writing a functional spec for a product until after the product ships; it's the only way I can ensure that the product matches the spec.

This book is based on release candidates 0 and 1 of the Beta 3 version of Windows 2000.

I've written this book using release candidates 0 and 1 of the Beta 3 version of Windows 2000. I guarantee, with absolute 100% certainty, that some features and operations of COM+ will change between this writing and the actual release of the software—new features might be added, scheduled features removed, operation of existing features modified. For example, as I write these words, a cool new feature has just been added that allows queued components (Chapter 4) to transmit persistent objects (objects that support the *IPersistStream* interface) as parameters to a queued COM call. This feature wasn't in Beta 2 or Beta 3 RC0. The team wanted to add it but didn't know if they would have time before Windows 2000 finally locked down. Delays in other portions of Windows 2000 gave them the time they needed to get it done.

We'll have to hustle to get its description into this book, as Chapter 4 has already gone to composition. The next feature change, whatever it is, may not make it into this edition. This text is more conceptual and less code-based than my previous books, which I hope will make it less vulnerable to late-breaking feature changes. I'm confident that the broad concepts and major architectural elements won't change. (And the timing constraints provide a perfect excuse for all the inaccuracies that inevitably creep into any software book.)

Go and Study

The Talmud speaks of the impatient man who came to the famous rabbi Hillel, saying, "Teach me the Torah while I stand on one foot." Hillel thought a moment and said, "What you do not want done to yourself, do not do to others. The rest is commentary, go and study." I hope you can stand on one foot long enough to read the following: COM+ provides the prefabricated services that you need to employ COM applications on an enterprise scale. The rest is commentary. I hope you enjoy reading it.

COM+ provides the prefabricated services that you need to employ COM applications on an enterprise scale.

Chapter Two

COM+ System Architecture

Business Problem Background

Writing enterprise applications requires us to solve completely different problems than does writing desktop applications. Suppose we want to take the business logic of Quicken, which increments or decrements a checking account, and scale it to the enterprise level to produce an electronic check payment system capable of handling many clients. What new types of problems would we have to solve, and what types of infrastructure would we have to add to that relatively simple business logic?

Our new enterprise application cares about security. We didn't care about security on the desktop, or more accurately, our customers didn't: they felt that if they kept their computers locked up in their houses, no one could get in to steal their money. Paranoid users could password-protect their PCs to keep unauthorized users from logging on, but hardly anyone did this. However, our enterprise application probably has dozens of users coming and going over the network. We need to ensure that we can definitively identify a remote customer and that she can make withdrawals from only her own account. We also need a way to identify administrative users, such as customer service personnel, who need access to all customer accounts. Finally, we need a way to administer the security system, to specify who is and is not allowed to perform which operations.

An enterprise application cares about security.

Another problem encountered in enterprise applications is synchronization. Since actions are initiated by sometimes hundreds of remote users instead of a single desktop user, problems can arise when two clients call a method on the same object at the same time. The operating system preemptively swaps between the two calls at indeterminate intervals, which means that one client's work can mess up another's. Think what happens when you are trying to cook Kung Pao chicken in the kitchen while your roommate is trying to make her grandmother's famous lasagna. We need some way to be sure that different operations don't mix hoisin sauce in the mozzarella cheese while still maintaining reasonable efficiency. It's difficult but possible to do this on a single desktop, because COM can use the Microsoft Windows message-queuing mechanism to schedule calls in sequence. However, once an application's functionality spans more than one machine and this mechanism is no longer available, it's extremely difficult and expensive to write code for all possible conditions that will keep different threads from tying themselves into a five-dimensional hyperpretzel.

System integrity is such a large problem that the entire next chapter, "Transactions," is devoted to it.

These are just a few of the problems faced by developers of enterprise applications. All of these problems deal with infrastructure and have nothing to do with incrementing or decrementing accounts, the business logic of our application. You know your business logic better than anyone else; that's why you went into the business of writing software to implement it. Writing the infrastructure required to solve these problems on an enterprise scale would mean that you'd never get the job done. It would take too long and cost too much, and your application programmers might not have the skills or experience. We need a way to separate the business logic from the infrastructure that it requires to operate on an enterprise scale. What we want ideally is a way to write our business logic and to inherit the infrastructure, to plug in somehow to an operating system that provides the infrastructure and other useful features.

Solution Architecture

In engineering school, I shared an office with a very religious fellow. He had a sign on his wall that read, "Let go, and let God." It pithily expressed his sincerely held worldview that if he got up every day and did his best at the things under his control (exams, problem sets, labs—his "business logic" at the time), God would handle the things beyond his control (keeping the stars in their courses, dispensing tidal waves and IRS audits), and that as a result of their joint effort, the universe would unfold the way it should. His philosophy required a relatively small amount of direct interaction with God (professions of belief, making of joyful noises, the occasional lamentation), and a large amount of living day-to-day life in the manner he believed was compatible with God's laws (being honest, giving to charity, searching for a wife who shared these values). Neither the direct nor indirect requirements were especially difficult, and this philosophy about the division of labor in the universe allowed him to cope with the complexities of life.

The slogan of the developers who first wrote Microsoft Transaction Server (MTS), which evolved into COM+, was "Let go, and let Viper [the early code-name for MTS]." Their basic idea was to separate an application's business logic, which varies greatly from one application to another, from the enterprise infrastructure, which doesn't. You write the business logic, packaging it in the form of COM components, and inherit the enterprise infrastructure from COM+. These components need a relatively small amount of direct interaction with COM+. For example, you must profess your belief in COM+ by installing your components into the COM+ run-time environment, as described later in this chapter. Your components must make joyful noises unto COM+ when they successfully complete a transaction, or lamentations when they abort a transaction, as discussed in Chapter 3. Your components must then live their lives, performing their business logic, in a manner compatible with the laws of COM+; for example,

Enterprise applications, like people, find the world overwhelming if they worry about everything that goes on in it.

The key to a happy life, for applications as well as people, is to restrict the set of things you worry about.

COM+ allows you to let go of all those overwhelming problems so you can devote your resources to handling your business logic.

by frequently releasing resources they no longer need (giving alms to less fortunate components). Neither the direct nor indirect requirements of living according to COM+'s laws are especially difficult. And if you do all of these things, then yea, verily, the COM+ run-time environment will wrap your components up in its loving arms and keep them safe from the nasty world that they can't control. Between the efforts of COM+ and those of your components, your business process will unfold as it should.

What are the drawbacks to such an approach? As with any higher level of abstraction, the primary drawback is loss of control. Granted, the operating system is doing things for you that you otherwise would have had to write yourself, but it is doing these things in a way that Microsoft has decided is the best fit for the greatest number of applications. This inherited infrastructure probably won't fit your specific project as perfectly as one you would custom craft yourself, if you could afford the time and effort. But you can't, of course. Your competitors who are letting go and letting COM+ will get to market so far ahead of you that you might as well not bother getting started. Thomas Lynch, poet and funeral director, wrote in *The Undertaking: Life Studies from the Dismal Trade* (Penguin, 1998) that letting go and letting God is "…a leap into the unknown where we are not in control but always welcome." That's as good a bumper-sticker description of COM+ as I've been able to craft.

Instead of writing your own security code to identify users, you can administratively tell COM+ that your component wants to receive calls only from certain users.

For example, instead of writing your own security code to identify users, you can administratively tell COM+ that your component wants to receive calls only from certain users. The COM+ run-time environment handles the task of authenticating these users and determining whether they belong to the allowed group. The administrative tools for specifying which users are allowed to call into your component are likewise part of COM+. You've let go and let COM+.

COM+ performs its magic by *interception*. Consider the operation of classic COM. A client application creates an object from a server by calling *CoCreateInstance* in C++ or by using the *new* operator in Visual Basic or Visual J++. If the client lives in the same machine, address space, and apartment as the server, the client application receives a direct connection to the object, as shown in Figure 2-1.

Figure 2-1 *A direct connection to an object in the same machine, address space, and apartment as the client.*

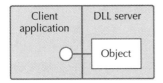

If the object lives anywhere else, the client receives an interface proxy instead, as shown in Figure 2-2. This proxy connects to a system-provided object called the remote procedure call (RPC) channel and thence to a stub on the server side. When the client makes a call, the proxy uses the RPC channel to squirt the call and its parameters across the process or machine boundary to the stub, which then makes the call to the object in the object's own address space. Neither client nor server has to think very much about the location of the other. So even classic COM provides a sort of transparent divine intervention working for you in every

COM+ performs its magic by interposing itself between client and server, pre- and post-processing method calls.

Figure 2-2 *A proxy/stub indirect connection to an object living somewhere else.*

Machine, process, or apartment boundary

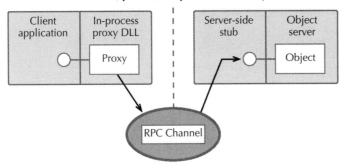

call, performing the very useful function of abstracting away the differences between the location of the client and the server. COM+ simply adds more functionality to this useful architecture.

Versions 1 and 2 of Microsoft Transaction Server provided their services as a separate wrapper on top of COM. When a client application created an object in the MTS environment, MTS created a separate object called a *context wrapper* and inserted it between the server-side stub and the actual object, as shown in Figure 2-3. All calls to the object had to pass through this context wrapper, in which MTS performed its abstraction mechanisms, such as security checking. The context wrapper also provided the storage area for MTS-specific information, such as the transaction to which the call belonged.

Figure 2-3 *A context wrapper as a separate layer in Microsoft Transaction Server versions 1 and 2.*

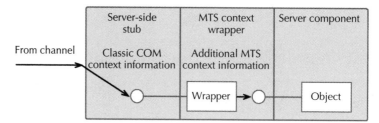

COM+ fuses together the functionality of MTS and classic COM. Because they are now unified internally, a separate wrapper layer is no longer used. The interception takes place on the client side between the proxy and the channel, and on the server side between the channel and the stub, as shown in Figure 2-4. When the proxy and stub are first attached to the new object, COM+ sets up the *policy objects* that its administrative information tells it should be in place for the object the client created.

The chain of policy objects on the client side is invoked when a method is called, and again after it returns. The chain of policy objects on the server side is invoked when the call first arrives on the server side, and again before it leaves. For example, if a server-

Figure 2-4 *Interception by policy objects in COM+.*

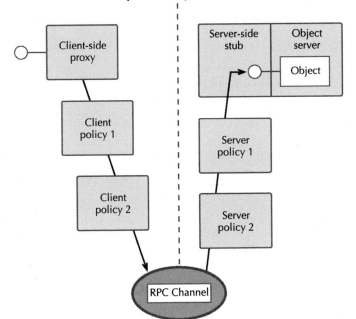

side component has been administratively designated as requiring synchronization, the server-side policy object might acquire a lock, such as a mutex, on entry and release the lock when it exits. The chain of policy objects is currently available only to the operating system; at this point, you cannot add your own policies to the chain.

Simplest COM+ Example

Let's consider the simplest example I can think of. COM+ requires its objects to be supplied in the form of components, which are dynamic link libraries (DLLs), described in more detail later in this chapter. Components provided in DLLs are able to run in the process address space of the client application that creates them, hence the name *in-proc* objects. Sometimes a client application wants an object to live in a different process outside the client's

COM+ provides many useful run-time services in response to settings made by an administrator rather than to code written by a vendor.

address space, either because the object lives on another machine or because the client application doesn't trust the object enough to let it inside. Normally an *out-of-proc* object would be provided by a separate executable COM server. The vendor of such a server would have to write the extra code required for that type of host; for example, to shut down the server program when its last object was released. Now COM+ provides the ability to wrap its own host process around the component DLL, thereby providing the benefits (and drawbacks, but that's life) of living outside a client's address space without the vendor having to write code for it. The system administrator makes settings using COM+'s administrative tools, and the COM+ run-time environment provides a surrogate process that hosts the component. We've let go, and let COM+.

The point of this chapter is to delineate which portions of the total operation of the sample application are written by you and which portions are provided by the operating system in response to your administrative settings. The rest of this book is about tapping into the different useful operations COM+ can perform on your behalf.

A COM+ workflow example begins here.

I've provided a sample component and client application, called Pinger, available on this book's Web site. The component's *ProgID* is *PingComponent.Pinger*. It exposes a single method called *Ping*, which does nothing except return a success code. A client application can use this component to measure call overhead on the same machine or over a network. The sample client application is shown in Figure 2-5. The terms *client* and *server* can get ambiguous very quickly in multitier programming, so we call this client application the *base client* because it resides at the base of the entire interaction. The user enters the number of calls to the *Ping* method that she wants the base client application to make. When the user clicks the Do It button, the client application creates an instance of the provided component, makes the specified number of calls to the *Ping* method, and displays the total elapsed time in milliseconds.

Figure 2-5 *The Pinger sample base client application.*

When the client creates an instance of the *Pinger* component, we want COM+ to launch the server in a separate process, so we first have to make administrative settings to tell COM+ this is what we want it to do. COM+ keeps all of its administrative settings in the COM+ catalog, a system database. The operation of this catalog is described in more detail later in this chapter. We make these administrative settings by using the Component Services snap-in, shown in Figure 2-6. This is a utility application, hosted inside

COM+ administrative settings are stored in the COM+ catalog.

We make entries in the COM+ catalog through the Component Services snap-in.

Figure 2-6 *The Component Services snap-in showing the Pinger sample application.*

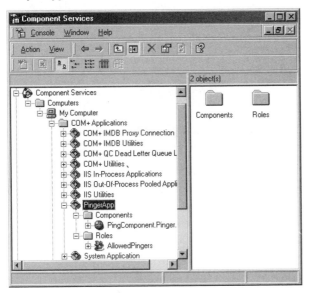

Microsoft Management Console (MMC), that provides system administrators with easy access to the COM+ catalog. All of the functionality provided to human administrators by the snap-in is also available to administrative programs through a series of system-provided utility objects, as described in the "COM+ Components" section of this chapter.

The main administrative unit of COM+ is an application, formerly known as a package.

The main administrative unit of COM+ is called an *application*. An application, in the COM+ sense of the word, is a set of administrative data containing information used by the COM+ infrastructure about a collection of components that work together. Unfortunately, using *application* in this context adds yet another meaning to a highly overloaded term. This set of administrative data is called a *package* in MTS. At first I hated the COM+ nomenclature, feeling that *package* communicated well the fact that this set of data is assembled administratively instead of compiled by a programmer into a single .EXE. On the other hand, the COM+ team deliberately chose *application* to indicate that this administrative data is self-contained, having within it all the elements necessary to get work done, such as components, type libraries, and registry settings. A simple .EXE generally is not self-contained in this manner, as anyone who has ever tried to move programs from one directory to another has discovered. The term is growing on me at least a little. Besides, *application* is used consistently throughout the COM+ user interface, so we'll all have to get used to it.

COM+ applications can run either as a separate process (a server application) or in the client application's address space (a library application).

You will find instructions for creating a new application in the sample code directory on this book's Web site. In Figure 2-6, I called the new application PingerApp. In this example we will deal only with the sample application's activation and shutdown settings. The first choice the designer of an application must make is whether to activate it as a *server application* or as a *library application*. The former runs in a separate address space from the client application, on either the same machine or a different machine, similar to a standard .EXE server in classic COM. The latter runs in the same address space as the client application, similar to a DLL server in classic COM. This difference is illustrated in Figures 2-7 and 2-8. The sample instructions tell you to make this choice, using the user interface shown in Figure 2-9.

A COM+ application contains components. A *component* is a COM object server packaged in a DLL. You write components to implement your business logic. You then use the Component Services snap-in to add your components to a COM+ application. This

A COM+ application is made up of components.

Figure 2-7 *A server application, which runs in a separate address space.*

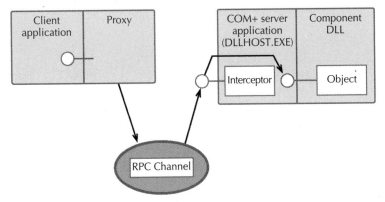

Figure 2-8 *A library application, which runs in the client application's address space.*

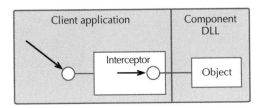

Figure 2-9 ***The user interface for selecting an activation type.***

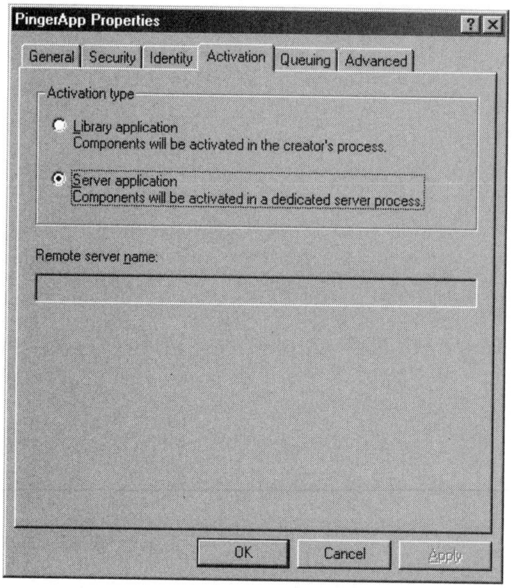

tells COM+ to make entries in its catalog to associate the component with the specified COM+ application and to remember the administrative properties you specify for the component—for example, whether it uses transactions, whether it can be pooled, which users are allowed to access it. I will discuss these properties in more detail elsewhere. For now, just concentrate on the fact that the component lives in the specified application. The sample code instructions will tell you to register the *Pinger* component and to place it into the application that you created for it.

Each component can live in only one application.

Each component can live in only one application. If you have a component that you want to be used by more than one program, you can place it in a library application. Different server applications (separate .EXEs) can use the same library application, each in their own process, as shown in Figure 2-10. An example of this is the COM+ Utilities application.

Figure 2-10 *Two server applications reusing components by means of a library application.*

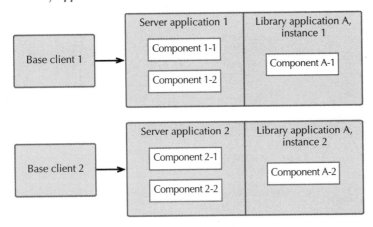

In the Pinger application, when the user clicks the Do It button, the sample base client application creates the *Pinger* object and calls its *Ping* method. The client application does not know or care whether this object uses COM+ services or not. It simply uses the operating system's standard object creation functions, in this case *CreateObject*. This function and all the rest of the operating system's COM infrastructure have now been updated to use COM+. When the client calls *CreateObject*, COM+ goes to its catalog and looks up the requested component. It sees that the component has indeed been installed as a COM+ component inside the sample application, and that this application has been configured to run as a server application. So COM+ launches a new process (using DLLHOST.EXE, the standard surrogate that appeared in Windows NT 4.0 service pack 2) and creates the *Pinger* object inside it. This operation is shown in Figure 2-11.

COM+ checks the component's server type settings when the base client creates it.

When does the new process containing our object shut down? In classic COM, you had to code whatever server lifetime behavior you thought your customers wanted to buy. With COM+,

COM+ provides, among many other services, lifetime management for server applications.

Figure 2-11 *A client application creating a COM+ object.*

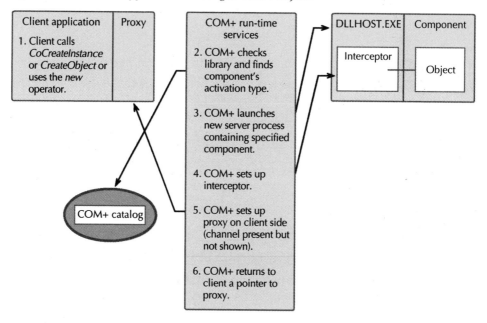

Client application	Proxy		COM+ run-time services		DLLHOST.EXE	Component

Client application / Proxy box:
1. Client calls *CoCreateInstance* or *CreateObject* or uses the *new* operator.

COM+ run-time services box:
2. COM+ checks library and finds component's activation type.

3. COM+ launches new server process containing specified component.

4. COM+ sets up interceptor.

5. COM+ sets up proxy on client side (channel present but not shown).

6. COM+ returns to client a pointer to proxy.

DLLHOST.EXE / Component box:
Interceptor | Object

COM+ catalog

the run-time services of the operating system control the lifetime of the server process according to administrative information that you provide. In Figure 2-12, you can see the Component Services snap-in asking how long the server is to run after its last object is destroyed. You can choose to have COM+ shut down the application when the last object has been gone for a specified amount of time, or you can leave the application running even when it has no objects to service and have an administrator shut it down. Here is another useful service you can inherit from the COM+ run time instead of having to code it yourself. This is just the first of many examples of letting go and letting COM+.

Figure 2-12 *Specifying the amount of time after which to shut down an idle COM+ server application.*

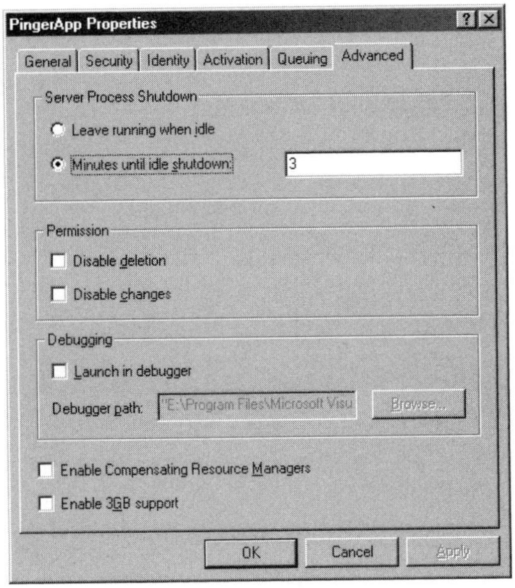

COM+ Components

A component is the software implementation of your business logic. It is the code that you write to accomplish the tasks that your customers are paying you to get done. It is the basic unit of software functionality in COM+, as an application is the basic unit of administration.

> A component is the basic unit of software functionality in COM+.

COM+ components are quite easy to produce in essentially any mainstream COM development environment, such as Microsoft Visual Basic, Microsoft Visual J++, or the Microsoft Visual C++ Active Template Library (ATL). Naturally, the development environments use slightly different names, but the components they create are really the same. In Visual Basic, components live in an ActiveX DLL. In Visual J++, they reside in a COM DLL, and in the Visual C++ ATL, they live in a DLL server.

What exactly constitutes
a component suffers
from a great deal of
ambiguity caused by
careless use of the term.

Unfortunately, further specification of what exactly constitutes a component suffers from a great deal of ambiguity caused by careless use of the term. I would love to give you a firm definition and say, "Component means this and nothing else," but no exclusive definition would hold true in the discussions you will see in the documentation and in the press. I'll describe for you here the nomenclature that I think makes sense, that matches the COM+ user interface better than any other, and which I will use consistently throughout this book.

Component seems to have three different and mutually contradictory usages in the current idiom. First, *component* is used to identify a DLL server that provides COM objects to the world. In this sense, *component* is synonymous with *DLL server* and *in-proc server*—although I'd suggest avoiding the latter as a generic term because, as we saw in the example earlier, the component DLL server will frequently be loaded into a process different from that of the client application. Documentation that states, "Your component should contain a type library," is using this meaning. I will not use *component* as a noun in this sense. When I want to speak of a DLL containing components, I will use the term as an adjective, for example, *component file* or *component DLL*.

As used in this book,
component means *class*.

The second usage of *component* is synonymous with *class*. It indicates a type of object, a species, of which you can create individual instances. In the real world, *cat* is a class, and my pet Simba is an instance of this class, an *object*. When you look at the Components folder within a COM+ application in the Component Services snap-in, every entry you see is a component in this sense of the word. I prefer this usage and wish it were used consistently throughout the universe. It makes sense to me and matches the user interface most closely. This is my meaning when I use *component* as a noun throughout this book. You develop a component; you install a component into the COM+ catalog.

The third usage of *component* is synonymous with *object*, as if object needed yet another definition. A component in this sense means an individual instance of a class. When documentation states, "To create a queued component, use *CoGetObject*," it is using this meaning. I will not use this meaning for component in this book or out of it, and urge you not to do so either. It buys you nothing and muddies the waters for everyone else. Whenever I want to indicate an individual instance of a class, I will use *object*—you instantiate an object, you call methods on an object.

COM+ requires your components (remember, this means classes) to be packaged in COM DLL servers. You can have more than one component per DLL. Components hosted from DLLs are much more versatile than those hosted from .EXE servers. For example, DLL-hosted components can live in or out of their clients' address space, whereas those packaged in .EXE servers must live in their own address space. COM+ would not be able to provide all of its services if it allowed you to package your components in .EXE servers.

COM+ components must be packaged in DLLs.

In order to work properly with the administrative and deployment utilities of COM+, your components should be self-registering. That is to say, the DLL in which they live should export the *Dll-RegisterServer* function, which, when called by a utility application, makes the standard registry entries needed by all COM classes. To be a good citizen, make sure that your components are self-unregistering as well, via the *DllUnregisterServer* function. Your development environment will often provide these capabilities for your component.

COM+ components should be self-registering.

All the interfaces and methods of your COM+ component should be described in a type library. You might get a component that lacks one to totter to its feet and say, "Hello, world"; however, so many features of COM+, such as queued components, events, and role-based security, will not work at all without a type library that you should consider it mandatory. For logistical convenience when deploying your component on its server machine(s), you'll probably want to bind the type library into the DLL that contains your component. However, you might find that keeping a separate

COM+ components should be described in a type library.

copy of the type library is also a good idea. For example, if you use a type library for marshaling, you might want to install only the type library, and not the DLL containing the actual component, on each client machine. Some development environments, such as the ATL, produce both bound and separate type libraries. The Enterprise Edition of Visual Basic will do this if you choose the Remote Server Files project option, but other editions provide only the bound version.

COM+ components will one day carry their administrative settings in component libraries.

A few pieces of COM+ administrative information, such as transaction requirement settings, have made their way into the existing type library format. However, the existing type library format is too restrictive to contain administrative settings that describe other COM+ features. COM+ components can carry this administrative data in a data structure called a *component library*. This is conceptually similar to a type library but contains different types of information. For example, the developer of a component can bind into that component the administrative data specifying which users can call the component's methods. Since there is at the time of this writing no commercially available development environment capable of producing a component library, I won't deal with it any further. But keep your eyes open—it's coming.

Since their objects will frequently live in different processes or machines from their clients, your components must provide support for marshaling their interfaces. If your interfaces are automation compatible, you can do this with the type library that your component DLL contains. If not, you must provide a proxy/stub generator DLL for marshaling your interfaces.

The COM+ Catalog

COM+ stores its administrative information in the COM+ catalog.

You've seen that COM+ requires a great deal of administrative information to work its magic behind the scenes; for example, it needs to know the COM+ application to which a component belongs. Classic COM required much less administrative information and stored it in the system registry. The amount of information required by COM+ demanded a new mechanism for storing and accessing it: a system database called the COM+ catalog (hereafter, simply the catalog).

The catalog is administered through a hierarchy of system-provided utility objects, all of which support scripting and remoting. These utility objects are available to any administrative application that you write. The Component Services snap-in is simply a convenient user interface placed on top of these system-provided objects.

> The Component Services snap-in is simply a utility for manipulating system-supplied catalog objects.

Top-level access to the catalog is provided through a component called the *COMAdminCatalog*, whose program ID is *COMAdmin*.*COMAdminCatalog*. I've listed this component's methods and their descriptions in Table 2-1. An administrative program that wants to use the catalog would simply create an object of this class and call its methods. Many of the context menu items you see when you right-click My Computer in the Component Services snap-in, such as Start IMDB, Stop IMDB, and Refresh All Components, are direct calls to this component's methods.

> The entry point to managing the COM+ catalog is provided by an component called the *COMAdminCatalog*.

The hierarchy of COM+ catalog administrative objects is shown in Figure 2-13. As you saw in Figure 2-6, the object hierarchy presented in the Component Services snap-in matches it in some places but not in others. For example, the snap-in displays the *Applications* collection but not the *InprocServers* collection. The designers of the Component Services snap-in provided access to the features that they thought would make sense to administrators, rather than directly exposing the underlying hierarchy without regard to the audience. This is good user interface design, as promoted by Alan Cooper in his classic book *About Face: The Essentials of User Interface Design* (IDG Press Worldwide, 1995), which I recommend highly.

> The COM+ catalog provides a hierarchy of data objects.

Table 2-1 *COMAdminCatalog* **Component Methods[1]**

Method	Description
Administrative Methods	
Connect	Connects to another computer and retrieves its "root" catalog collection
GetCollectionByQuery	Retrieves any collection anywhere in the hierarchy
Application Methods	
ExportApplication	Writes information about an application to an .MSI file for transmittal to another machine
InstallApplication	Reads and imports an application .MSI file and installs the application onto the local machine
ShutdownApplication	Manually shuts down a COM+ server application running on the catalog's machine
StartApplication	Manually starts a COM+ application running on the catalog's machine
Component Methods	
GetMultipleComponentsInfo	Gets information from the COM+ catalog about one or more registered components
ImportComponent	Places a component that is already registered as an in-proc COM component into the COM+ catalog
InstallComponent	Places a single component that is *not yet* registered as an in-proc COM component into the COM+ catalog
InstallMultipleComponents	Places multiple components that are *not yet* registered as in-proc COM components into the COM+ catalog
RefreshComponents	Refreshes the COM+ information about all registered components
In-Memory Database Methods	
StartIMDB	Starts the In-Memory Database service
StopIMDB	Stops the In-Memory Database service
Load-Balancing Methods	
RefreshRouter	Refreshes performance data used by load-balancing service
StartRouter	Starts the load-balancing router service
StopRouter	Stops the load-balancing router service

1. As this book goes to press, additional administrative methods, as well as sets of Event Class and Backup/Restore methods, have been developed.

Figure 2-13   *The COM+ catalog administrative object hierarchy.*

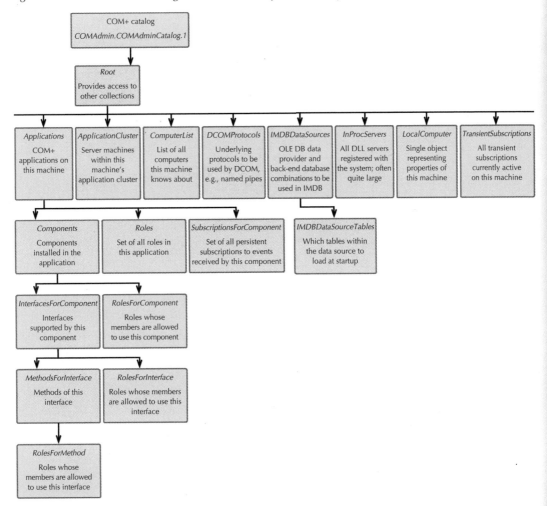

Besides having its own methods, the *COMAdminCatalog* component nent exposes the *GetCollection* method to provide access to a series of collections of subobjects. Each collection is represented by an object of the *COMAdminCatalogCollection* component; its methods are shown in Table 2-2. The *COMAdminCatalogCollection* component contains such methods as *Add* and *Remove*, for creating or destroying an object from the collection, as well as *GetCollection*, to access a subcollection within it. The collection

Table 2-2   Selected Methods of the
COMAdminCatalogCollection Component

Method	Description
Element Manipulation Methods	
Add	Adds a new element to the collection and returns a reference to the new element
Remove	Removes a specified element from the collection
SaveChanges	Saves all changes made to elements in the collection into the catalog
Methods for Populating the Collection with Data	
Populate	Reads in data for all objects in this collection
PopulateByKey	Reads in data for only specified objects in this collection
PopulateByQuery	Reserved for future use
Subcollection Access Method	
GetCollection	Accesses a subcollection belonging to an object from the main collection—for example, the *Components* collection belonging to an application

labeled *Root* is a special case. It exists solely to provide access to the collections under it. It contains no properties or other objects.

Each object in a collection contains properties that apply to that type of object. For example, every element of the *Applications* collection is an application object. It has properties such as *Name*—in this example, *Pinger*. The Pinger sample earlier in this chapter contained a property called *ShutdownAfter*, the amount of time after which the idle application should be shut down. Some properties are read-only and some are read-write, which should be familiar. Other properties are write-once, for example the *ID* property of an application, which represents the globally unique identifier (GUID) for a particular COM+ application. It is cleared by the catalog when you create a new application. You then set it to the desired value, as for any other property, but after that, the system will not allow you to change it. If you can't live with your initial selection, you have to delete it and add it again. Other properties, such as the application's *Password* property, have the curious attribute of being write-only. You can change them all you want, but you can never find out the value they currently hold. Only the operating system has read access for these properties.

Each object in the catalog represents a unit of COM+ administrative data.

Using the catalog's administrative objects is pretty simple. For example, to add a new application to your computer, you would use the standard object creation functions to create the catalog object to gain access to the catalog system. You would call the catalog's *GetCollection* method to gain access to the *Root* collection, and then call the collection's *GetCollection* method to gain access to the *Applications* collection. You would call this collection's *Add* method to create a new application within the collection. Finally, you would call the methods on the new application object to set its properties to the values that you wanted. This process is shown in Figure 2-14.

Figure 2-14 *Adding a new application to the catalog.*

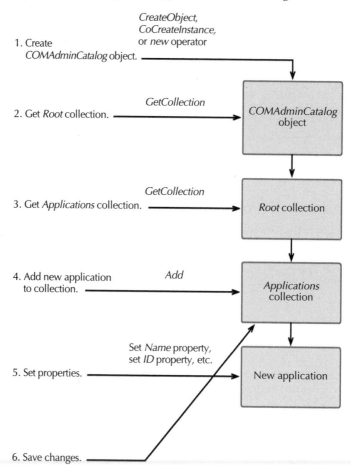

1. Create
   COMAdminCatalog object.

   *CreateObject,
   CoCreateInstance,
   or new operator*

   **COMAdminCatalog
   object**

2. Get *Root* collection.

   GetCollection

   Root collection

3. Get *Applications* collection.

   GetCollection

   **Applications
   collection**

4. Add new application
   to collection.

   Add

5. Set properties.

   Set *Name* property,
   set *ID* property, etc.

   New application

6. Save changes.

COM+ Context

An object's context is the COM+ environment in which it lives.

The COM+ run-time environment is much richer than that of classic COM. The operating system supplies many more features that you can use administratively instead of by writing code. For example, a COM+ object might or might not be participating in a transaction. It might or might not be making use of COM+'s synchronization or security services. The data that COM+ uses to keep track of exactly what each object is currently up to is referred to as an object's *context.* It represents the environment in which an individual object lives, the sea in which it swims.

An object's context is created and attached to the object by COM+ when COM+ activates the object. If a component does not allow object pooling (see Chapter 3), activation occurs when the object is first created. If a component does allow object pooling, activation occurs when an object is fetched from the pool. Once an object's context is created and attached to the object, the context is fixed and immutable until the object is deactivated—either destroyed (in the case of nonpooled objects) or returned to the pool (pooled objects).

An object's context is created and attached to the object by COM+ when COM+ activates the object.

When creating the context for an object, COM+ looks at the component's catalog entries to determine which attributes to place in the context. COM+ also considers the context of the creator, the object from which the creation request originates. For example, a component specifies whether its objects must live within a transaction. Based on these settings and the transaction (if any) to which the object's creator belongs, COM+ creates a new object in the transaction of that creator, in a new transaction, or in no transaction. Once this decision has been made, the new object is stuck with it for the rest of its active lifetime.

When creating the context for an object, COM+ looks at the component's catalog entries to determine which attributes to place in the context.

The context attributes specified by a component form part of its contract with its clients, in the same manner as do its interfaces. For example, you will write a component in a completely different way—and its clients will use it in a completely different way—when it requires a transaction compared with when it doesn't. And just as you do not change your components' interfaces without careful version control, neither do you want to change their context requirements without careful version control. Imagine the chaos if you installed a new version of a component and all of a sudden it required membership in a certain security group to access its methods. You better hope you haven't completely trashed the old version (and that you haven't sold a copy to the postal service).

The context information that accompanies every COM+ object lives in a separate container known as the *context object*. A context object is implicitly tied to the COM+ object that it describes.

The context information that accompanies every COM+ object lives in a separate container known as the *context object*.

Any COM+ object can access its accompanying context object to make its own use of this information. You will probably see the context object also referred to as the "object context." I think that calling it the context object differentiates well between the context itself (all the information COM+ maintains) and the object that represents the context to the world,—a logical view, if you will, of that information.

In MTS, an object called the *GetObjectContext* function to obtain the *IObjectContext* interface.

In MTS, an object obtained its context object by calling the *GetObjectContext* function, available in Visual C++, Visual Basic, and Visual J++. This call returned a pointer to the *IObjectContext* interface, whose methods are shown in Table 2-3. You can see that this interface is something of a hodgepodge. The security-related methods are discussed later in this chapter. The transaction-related methods are discussed in Chapter 3. The object creation method was used in MTS to explicitly flow existing context information into newly created objects. This method is no longer required because COM+ now does this automatically.

COM+ adds several new interfaces to make accessing an object's context easier and more powerful.

Several new interfaces have been added to the context object to make it easier and more logical to use. The *IObjectContextInfo* interface contains status information; its methods are listed in Table 2-4. The *IContextState* interface provides methods used for participating in transactions and just-in-time activation. It is discussed, and its methods listed, in Chapter 3. The *ISecurityCallContext* interface contains methods for handling security. Its methods are discussed later in this chapter in the "Security" section.

You can obtain any interface on the context object by calling *CoGetObjectContext* or by querying the *IObjectContext* interface.

The mechanisms used for obtaining these new interfaces are still evolving at the time of this writing. The *CoGetObjectContext* function, which will return any of these interface pointers directly, has been added to the Windows API. Plans for adding this function to Visual Basic and Visual J++ have not yet been announced, though I'd be astounded if this didn't happen quickly. Calling *GetObjectContext* will continue to work as before, returning the *IObjectContext* interface. You can obtain any other interface supported by the context object by querying (casting, for you Visual Basic and Visual J++ people) this interface.

Table 2-3 *IObjectContext* **Interface Methods**

Method	Description
Transaction Methods	
IsInTransaction	Indicates whether the object is in a transaction
SetComplete	Indicates component is done with its transactional work and happy with the result
SetAbort	Indicates component is done with its transactional work and unhappy with the result
EnableCommit	Indicates component hasn't necessarily finished its transactional work but is currently happy
DisableCommit	Indicates component hasn't finished its transactional work but is currently unhappy
Security Methods	
IsSecurityEnabled	Indicates whether COM+ security is turned on for this object
IsCallerInRole	Indicates whether the direct caller of an object method is a member of the specified role
Object Creation Method	
CreateInstance	Creates a new COM object within the current context; no longer needed in COM+

A context object is extensible, but the mechanisms for extending it have not been published. Various Microsoft environments can add information to the context object to describe the environment in which an object finds itself. For example, when Microsoft Internet Information Server (IIS) compiles an active server page, IIS adds to the context object certain "built-in" objects that represent the IIS environment functionality available for the use of the active server page (ASP) script. These objects include, for example, the *Request* object, which the ASP script can use for reading cookies from the client. The ASP script accesses these built-in IIS objects via the *IGetContextProperties* interface on its context object. Unfortunately, the mechanisms used for adding information to the context object have not been exposed or documented at the time of this writing, nor have any plans for doing so been announced by Microsoft.

Other Microsoft environments can add information to the context.

Table 2-4 *IObjectContextInfo* Interface Methods

Method	Description
GetActivityId	Returns the GUID that uniquely identifies synchronization activity to which caller belongs
GetContextId	Returns the GUID that uniquely identifies context to which caller belongs
GetTransaction	Returns the *ITransaction* interface of transaction to which caller belongs
GetTransactionId	Returns the GUID that uniquely identifies transaction to which caller belongs
IsInTransaction	Tells whether caller is or is not part of a transaction

Security

Security is vital to an enterprise application.

Security is vital to any distributed system. Unlike a desktop application, an enterprise application that doesn't care about security is unheard of. Obviously, applications that manipulate valuable data, such as the Sample Bank application in Chapter 3, need to ensure that users access only the data that they are supposed to. However, even those enterprise systems that provide only public information—for example, a product literature request system—still need a way to make sure that only administrators with the correct credentials are allowed to modify the materials that users can view. Desktop programmers often must fundamentally change their mindsets as they start scaling their desktop business logic and processes to the enterprise level.

Despite its importance, security often gets shortchanged in application development. Writing good security code is quite difficult and quite expensive. I shudder to think of the security holes we left in the foreign exchange application that I worked on years ago and discussed in Chapter 1. But we didn't know any better, and we couldn't have afforded the time or money even if we had.

COM+ lets you inherit a security infrastructure and get out of the security-coding business.

With the possible exception of transactions, the most widely useful feature of COM+ is its security infrastructure. COM+ saves you money by allowing your applications to inherit the security infrastructure that they need with almost no coding effort. By letting go and letting COM+, you can get out of the security-coding business.

Suppose a central pharmacy application in a hospital receives a call from a remote point-of-care application saying that Dr. Jones wants to prescribe morphine for a patient. The pharmacy application needs to answer definitively the two questions fundamental to all computer security before actually releasing the drug. First, is it really Dr. Jones on the other end? Maybe it's someone pretending to be Dr. Jones in order to steal valuable narcotics. Second, once we're satisfied that it really is Dr. Jones, is Dr. Jones allowed to prescribe morphine? Maybe her privileges in this hospital have expired. These two questions are answered respectively by the processes of *authentication* ("Are you really who you say you are?") and *authorization* ("Now that I know who you are, are you allowed to do what you are trying to do?").

Read this whole paragraph.

Authentication

Authentication is handled transparently by the operating system's Security Support Provider (SSP). Windows NT 4.0 has its own built-in SSP. Windows 2000 provides a standard interface, called SSPI, that allows vendors to develop and administrators to install different SSPs to match their business needs. One of these is Kerberos, a popular enterprise security provider that ships with Windows 2000. David Chappell's forthcoming book from Microsoft Press, *Understanding Microsoft Windows 2000 Distributed Services,* provides a good explanation of the functionality and architecture of the SSPI in Windows 2000.

Authentication is provided transparently by the operating system.

In order to use the operating system's authentication service, both client and server specify their desired *authentication levels.* These levels tell the operating system how hard you want it to work to ensure that an incoming call does indeed come from the authenticated party and that it hasn't been tampered with or spied on while in transit. COM+ server applications use administrative settings to specify their authentication levels, as shown in Figure 2-15. The client sets its own authentication level by calling the *CoInitialize-Security* function when it starts up. If the client and server specify different authentication levels, the operating system chooses the

If client and server specify different authentication levels, the operating system chooses the higher of the two.

higher of the two. Because it runs in the process of the client application, a library application does not have a choice; it always uses the authentication level specified by the client application for outgoing calls. The available authentication levels are shown in Table 2-5.

Figure 2-15 *Specifying the authentication level for a COM+ application.*

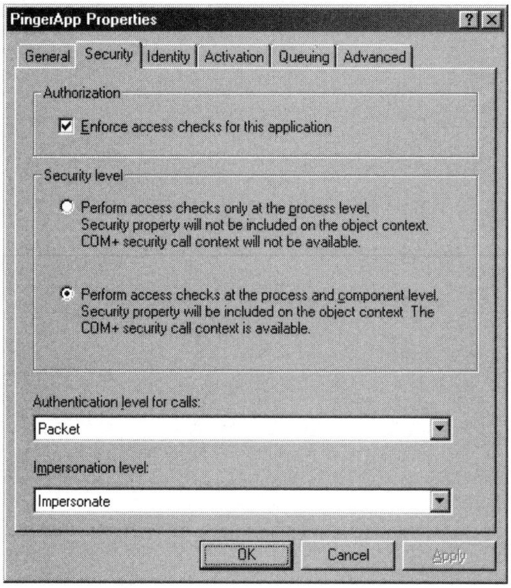

Here are a few pointers to keep in mind when choosing among the available authentication levels: Choosing no authentication means that you are allowing clients anonymous access to your server. Be sure that the operations that you allow through anonymous access can't mess anything up. Although you probably want to allow anonymous clients to read your advertising literature, you certainly don't want them to change it.

Encryption is growing in importance, but performing it with software can be slow.

The need for encryption is often underestimated. Unless you can physically secure every inch of wire in your enterprise application, and almost nobody can, anything you put on your network can wind up on the front page of the *New York Times*. This possibility could make you lean toward using the Packet Privacy authentication level because it automatically encrypts all the data to avoid eavesdropping. However, the overhead of software encryption will slow down your network communication, and if you find yourself using it very often, you should consider buying encrypted network cards. Hardware encryption is much faster than software encryption, and encrypted network cards don't cost much more to buy.

Authorization

Once you have set the authentication level, you can turn your attention to authorization—determining which users are allowed to perform a particular operation. Authorization depends, first of all, on authentication being set to at least the Call level. If you set your authentication level to None, you won't know who the caller is, which makes any kind of authorization pointless.

Authentication must be enabled for COM+ authorization to work.

Table 2-5   Authentication Levels in COM+

Level	Authentication	When to Use	Protects Against	Performance Cost
None	Nothing	Never	• Nothing	None
Connect	Check user ID	First connection of client and server	• Unauthorized user	Low
Call	Check user ID and encrypt sequence number	Every method call	• Unauthorized user • Recording/playback of network traffic	Low
Packet	Check user ID and encrypt sequence number	Every packet of every method call	• Unauthorized user • Recording/playback of network traffic	Low
Packet Integrity	Provide packet authentication level and encrypted checksum of data	Every packet of every method call	• Unauthorized user • Recording/playback of network traffic • Tampering	Medium
Packet Privacy	Provide packet integrity authentication level and encrypt all data	Every packet of every method call	• Unauthorized user • Recording/playback of network traffic • Tampering • Eavesdropping	Highest

The system administrator specifies roles for an application, which are basically user groups, and then assigns users to roles.

COM+ provides a prefabricated infrastructure for solving the problems of authorization. This infrastructure centers around the concept of a *role*, which is an application-wide group of users. Each application has its own collection of roles, which are named by alphanumeric strings such as Doctors, Nurses, Paramedics, or Administrators. Roles are stored in the COM+ catalog. The administrator uses the Component Services snap-in or another administrative application to add the roles to an application, in this case, Allowed Pingers, as previously shown in Figure 2-6. Users are assigned to roles by the administrator, as shown in Figure 2-16. The example shows that the administrator of the system is to be an Allowed Pinger.

Figure 2-16 *Assigning users to a role.*

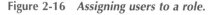

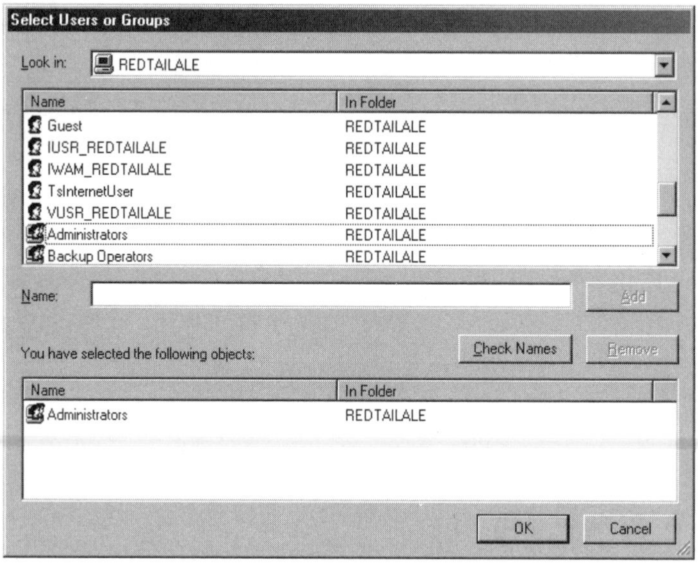

The easiest way to use role-based security is simply to refuse to allow any user who is not assigned to a particular role to create an object or call a method. COM+ allows an administrator to specify which components, interfaces, and methods can be accessed by members of which roles. The dialog box for doing this is shown in Figure 2-17.

Chapter Two

You can say, for example, that only base clients who are logged on and authenticated by the operating system as members of the Doctors role are allowed to call the *IPharmacy::PrescribeNarcotic* method. When a base client makes a method call to an object, the COM+ interceptor looks in the catalog to see which roles the caller has been assigned to. The interceptor then looks in the catalog to see whether the administrator has made the desired method available to members of these roles. If so, the call goes through. If not, the interceptor swallows the call and generates an administrative event to alert the system that someone has

COM+ can automatically restrict access to components to the members of specified roles.

Figure 2-17 *Specifying which components can be accessed by which roles.*

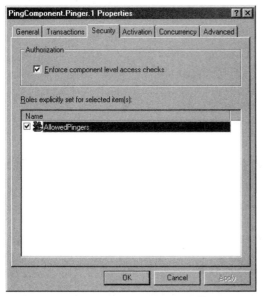

tried to step out of line. This process is shown in Figure 2-18. You can very easily add your own role-based security to the Pinger sample application.

You should be aware that administrative role checking as described above is performed only on calls from outside a COM+ application, either from a base client, as shown here, or from another COM+ application. All components within an application

Administrative role checking is only performed at COM+ application boundaries.

are required to trust one another, so COM+ doesn't waste time checking when component A calls component B within the same application. If you want role checking within an application, you must write it yourself, which isn't hard.

You can perform role checking within your application's business logic by using the *ISecurityCallContext* interface.

It would be nice to design all your interfaces so that all authorization questions could be handled administratively by the interceptor, as just discussed. Unfortunately, this granularity is too coarse for many needs. For example, depending on the drug selected by a doctor in a client application's user interface, the client application would need to know whether to call the *PrescribeNarcotic* method, which is restricted to licensed doctors, or the *Prescribe-OverTheCounterMed* method, which is available to any user. You don't want that logic to live in your client tier. What happens when a drug changes status, as have Ibuprofen and Rogaine?

Figure 2-18 *The process of administrative role checking in COM+.*

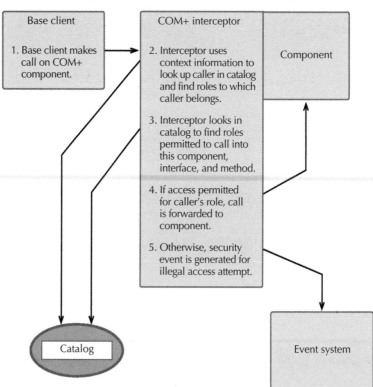

You would have to change every client application in the world, immediately. Instead, we want the ability to do role-based differentiation inside our components. To provide this capability, COM+ provides the *ISecurityCallContext* interface, whose methods are listed in Table 2-6. The *IsSecurityEnabled* method will tell you whether role-based security is turned on. The *IsCallerInRole* method will tell you whether the base client is a member of the role you specify. This process is shown in Figure 2-19. The *IObject-Context* interface also contains two methods with the same names that do the same thing.

The *IsSecurityEnabled* method will tell you whether role-based security is turned on and the *IsCallerInRole* method will tell you whether the base client is a member of the role you specify.

Figure 2-19 *The process of programmatic role checking in COM+.*

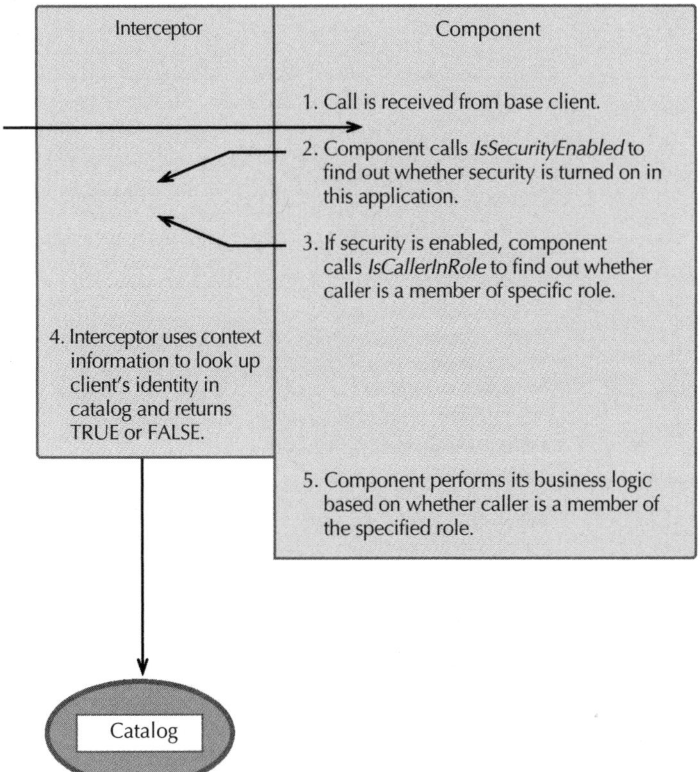

Table 2-6 *Selected ISecurityCallContext* **Interface Methods**

Method	Description
IsCallerInRole	Indicates whether the direct caller of an object method is a member of the specified role
IsSecurityEnabled	Indicates whether COM+ security is turned on for this object

The *ISecurityCallContext* interface also provides much more extensive security information. You access these items of information through the *Item* property of this interface, shown in Table 2-7. The additional items of security information available through this interface are listed in Table 2-8.

Even higher degrees of security information are available to your application if you want them.

What if even this level of security checking isn't enough? (Short answer: make it enough, because it's free.) COM+ provides even

Table 2-7 *ISecurityCallContext* **Interface Properties**

Property	Description
Count	Returns number of items in security call context
Item	Returns a specific item from the security call context

Table 2-8 *ISecurityCallContext* **Additional Items Available Through the *Item* Property**

Item	Description
Callers	Chain of all callers leading up to the present call
DirectCaller	Immediate caller of the object
MinAuthenticationLevel	Lowest authentication level used in the chain of calls
NumCallers	Number of callers in chain of calls to the object
OriginalCaller	Caller that originated the chain of calls on the object, the "base client"

finer-grained security information if you need it. The *ISecurity-Property* interface, obtained by querying the *IObjectContext* interface, will provide your object with the security IDs of its original creator (the base client), direct creator, original caller, and direct caller. You can then use security functions such as *AccessCheck* to see whether the caller you are interested in should be granted access to the resource you are guarding. The new COM+ *ISecurityCallContext* interface provides even more security information. Its methods will identify all of your object's upstream callers, not just the original and immediate ones. It will also give you the name of the authentication service and the authentication level currently in use.

Server Process Identity

Another administrative setting that you must specify for your COM+ server application is its *Identity*, using the Identity tab supplied by the Component Services snap-in shown in Figure 2-20. When a client application launches a COM+ server application by creating an object, which user's security credentials does the server have? For example, when the server tries to open a secured file and the operating system checks to see whether it is allowed to do so, against which user or group of users does the operating system check the server's credentials? Is it the user logged on to the client machine, the user logged on to the server machine, or some other user? Although the first of these possibilities is an option in classic DCOM, COM+ does not allow this sort of security check because of server scalability restrictions. The latter two choices are available to you in COM+.

You must choose which user ("security principal") your server application will run as.

If you choose Interactive User, your server process will run with the security credentials of whichever user happens to be logged on to the server machine. Choosing this option also makes all of your server application's user interface visible to the human sitting at the server machine, by far the best choice for debugging. The user interface is visible because the server application runs on the

You can configure your server application to run as the same user who is already logged on to the server machine.

Figure 2-20 *Setting the* Identity *property of a server application.*

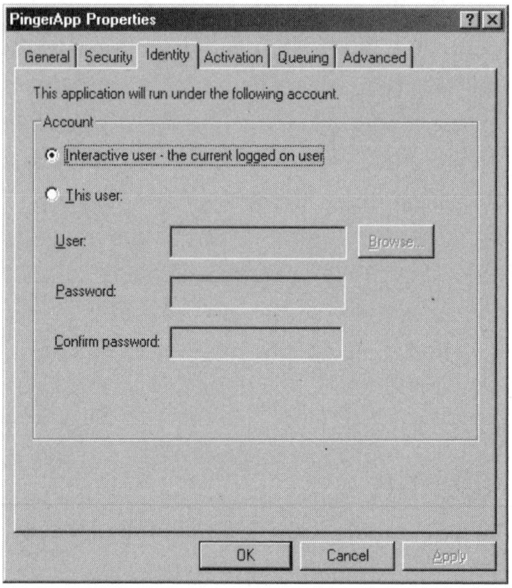

Think of a window station as a separate virtual machine.

interactive *window station.* A window station is an operating system abstraction representing a separate monitor, keyboard, and mouse, with a few other items like a clipboard and a running object table thrown in as well. If you think of a window station as a separate virtual machine, you won't be far off. More than one window station can exist on a computer at a time, but only one can be the interactive window station, the one whose virtual monitor, keyboard, and mouse are connected to the physical devices plugged in to your computer. However, running as the interactive user poses some drawbacks. If a client tries to launch a server process but no user is logged on to the server machine, the call will fail and your client will be angry. If the server process is successfully launched but the user then logs off, the server process will be terminated—angry client again. You usually choose this setting only for debugging.

Running as a specific user is probably a better idea for production environments. When the client launches a server application, the system creates the server process with the identity of the user specified in the catalog, regardless of who is logged on to the server machine. If the specified user is not currently logged on, the operating system creates a new noninteractive window station to run the server. The server's user interface will not be visible because its window station is not the interactive one. If the server pops up a dialog box, a user will not be able to see it or to press Enter to dismiss it because the keyboard is connected to the interactive window station as well. If the specified user is currently logged on, the process is created in the interactive window station. If the user later logs off, the window station is not destroyed, but merely made noninteractive; thus the server process doesn't terminate. This is a more robust approach than running as the interactive user.

Although the specific user account for an enterprise application looks and feels like an account for a human user, real-life installations generally provide a separate account for the use of each enterprise application. You don't just run your foreign-exchange trading-room application with the same identity as Charlie down the hall. That's why you will often see the identity of the server process referred to as the Security Principal, or sometimes Security Identity, rather than User ID.

Alternatively, you can configure your server application to run as a specific user, regardless of who is logged on to the server machine.

The identity of your server application becomes important when the application needs to access a remote database that cares about the identity of its users. For example, consider the prescription application discussed in the preceding section. The end user enters the prescription in the user interface, and then the object in the COM+ server application uses COM+'s security service to ensure that the user logged on to the machine is a member of the DoctorsWithCurrentNarcoticsLicenses role. The object enters the prescription into the database, using the server's own identity, not that of the remote client, as shown in Figure 2-21. The database trusts the middle-tier server to have done all the required security checking, so it doesn't bother with another layer of authorization. (You trust your wife to go through your wallet, so you don't bother asking her what she wants the money for.) This is called the *trusted-server* security model.

A three-tier COM+ system will work better if the database trusts the middle layer to perform all required security checking.

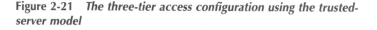
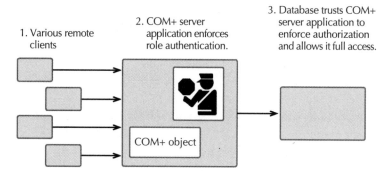

3. Database trusts COM+ server application to enforce authorization and allows it full access.

2. COM+ server application enforces role authentication.

1. Various remote clients

COM+ object

The database layer often contains security checks or audit trails that depend on the actual database entry being made under the network identity of the base client.

Not every database installation is comfortable with this approach. Many databases were designed and database administrators trained before three-tier programming became popular. Particularly with legacy systems, the database layer often contains security checks or audit trails that depend on the actual database entry being made under the network identity of the base client. This approach is shown in Figure 2-22. In this case, the server object *impersonates* the base client, temporarily taking on the base client's identity by means of the *CoImpersonateClient* function. The call from server object to database then proceeds with the base client's identity, not the server application's. The database does whatever

Figure 2-22 *The three-tier access configuration using the impersonation/delegation model.*

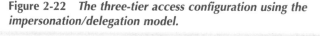
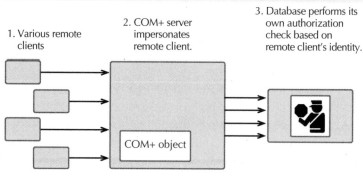

3. Database performs its own authorization check based on remote client's identity.

2. COM+ server impersonates remote client.

1. Various remote clients

COM+ object

authorization or auditing it wants to do, depending on the identity of the base client. This is called the *impersonation/delegation* security model.

While it might sound attractive, this approach is costly in terms of performance. It requires two authentications instead of one, the first when the server object impersonates the base client and the second when the database checks the server object's current impersonating identity. Furthermore, when an operation fails, it does so rather late in the process. You've already gone down three tiers instead of two and made two network hops instead of one. If you forget your wallet, it's better that you realize it when you arrive at the supermarket, rather than when you're in the checkout line. Finally, this approach loses the benefit of any type of connection pooling supported by the database. I would expect to see this approach used to connect COM+ middleware with legacy database systems, especially when the legacy database system has undergone extensive certification requirements that you don't want to lose.

The database can enforce security by having the middle layer impersonate the base client, but this is slow.

What happens when the database really needs the identity of the base client, perhaps to comply with a regulatory requirement for auditing? In this case, you can add a field to the database table, and the middle tier can explicitly pass the base client's identity.

Threading Apartments

COM and threading have always coexisted uneasily at best. Windows NT 3.1 introduced threads but didn't support 32-bit COM at all. Each subsequent version of Windows NT added another modality for supporting COM: version 3.5 allowed it on one thread per process, version 3.51 and Windows 95 introduced the single-threaded apartment model, and Windows NT 4.0 allowed tough objects to hold wild parties in the multithreaded apartment. Each model had its advantages and drawbacks, essentially getting

COM+ provides significant improvements in the handling of multithreaded COM programming.

harder to write as it got more powerful. As I carefully marshaled object references and worried about one apartment's residents not speaking to those of another, I wondered, "Why can't we all just get along?" Just as America or Eastern Europe carries the baggage of ethnic conflict from successive waves of immigration or conquest, so does COM carry the baggage of all the threading schemes hatched in different versions. COM+ finally provides a new type of apartment—the *neutral* apartment—that more or less gets along with everyone. COM+ also provides prefabricated support for object synchronization, removing the primary stumbling block to writing objects that perform well in a multithreaded environment. I will discuss the neutral apartment and synchronization in the following sections.

The Neutral Apartment

Read this whole paragraph.

To understand threading in COM+, you need to understand the concept of an apartment. An apartment is a logical container within a process for objects that share the same thread access requirements. Each object lives in one and only one apartment. The apartment in which an object lives determines the thread or threads on which it will receive its incoming calls.

A thread can enter and occupy a single-threaded apartment.

Every thread that wants to use COM must initialize COM by calling *CoInitializeEx*, passing either the *COINIT_APARTMENT-THREADED* flag or the *COINIT_MULTITHREADED* flag. A thread that does this is said to have *entered an apartment*, in which it will remain until it calls *CoUninitialize* or terminates. When a thread, say T1, calls *CoInitializeEx* and passes the *COINIT_APARTMENT-THREADED* flag, thread T1 is said to have created and entered a new *single-threaded apartment*, or STA. Think of it as a small studio apartment with room for only one thread, although it can contain any number of objects. All objects that are subsequently created in this new STA will receive their calls only on the thread that created the apartment, in this case, T1. A process can contain any number of STAs. If threads T1 and T2 each call *CoInitializeEx* and pass the *COINIT_APARTMENTTHREADED* flag, then each of these will create and enter a new STA. This is shown pictorially at the top of Figure 2-23.

A thread that calls *ColnitializeEx* and passes the *COINIT_MULTI-THREADED* flag is said to have entered the process's *multi-threaded apartment,* or MTA. A process contains only one MTA. Every thread that calls *ColnitializeEx* and passes this flag enters the same MTA. Think of it as a bunkroom that can sleep any number of backpackers if they don't mind being cozy. All objects that are subsequently created in the MTA can receive their calls on any thread that has entered the MTA. This is shown at the bottom of Figure 2-23.

Any number of threads can enter the multithreaded apartment.

The developer of a component specifies which type of apartment its objects can live in by adding the named value *ThreadingModel* to the component's *InProcServer* registry entry,

Components with thread affinity must reside in an STA.

Figure 2-23 *Objects living in apartments.*

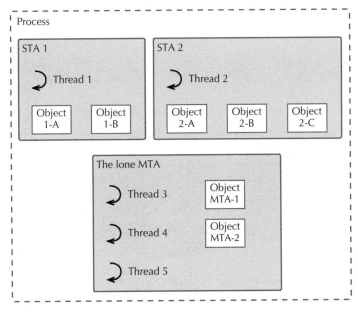

as shown in Figure 2-24. An entry of *Apartment* tells COM to create the object in an STA. An object that selects this entry is saying that it expects to receive all its calls from a single thread, the thread that created the STA. Since any window receives all its messages on the same thread, this is the best model for COM-based user interface code that makes use of windows. Since all calls will arrive on this thread only, the component developer has to write very little synchronization code. Furthermore, since every call arrives on the same thread, the component developer can use techniques that depend on thread affinity, such as keeping data in thread-local storage. Components developed with Visual Basic and the Microsoft Foundation Classes (MFC) do the latter and therefore must live in an STA.

Components without thread affinity will run more efficiently in the MTA than in an STA.

An entry of *Free* tells COM to create the object in the process's lone MTA, where it can party with anyone in the bunkroom, accepting calls on any thread that lives in the MTA. This is a good choice for worker components that don't have any user interface components. Since they are not tied to a specific window, there's no reason to tie them to a specific thread. Because this type of object can receive a call from any MTA thread at any time, it must provide its own synchronization code to ensure that concurrent accesses from different MTA threads do not cause any damage. Prior to Windows 2000, this requirement forced developers to write some extremely difficult code, which is why relatively few of these components are around. Now, however, COM+ offers the

Figure 2-24 *A registry entry specifying the component's apartment requirements.*

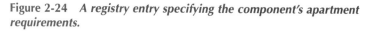

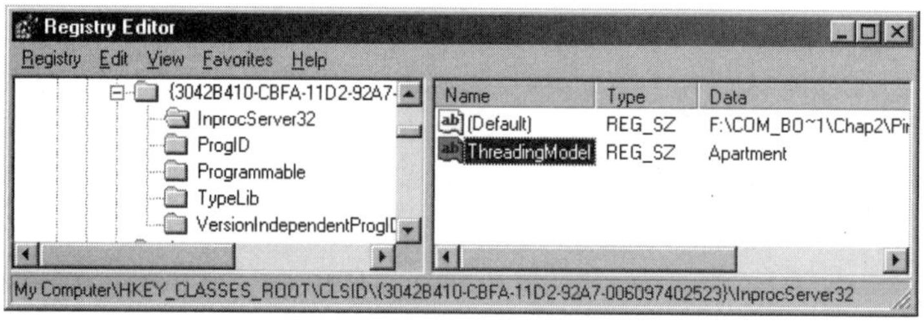

option of inheriting this synchronization from the operating system, as described in the next section.

The *Both* entry is misnamed; it really should be called *Either*. It tells COM that the object doesn't give a hoot which apartment it lives in: it is equally at home in an intimate studio with one thread or in the bunkroom with everyone. An object with this *ThreadingModel* entry is always created in the apartment of its creating thread.

The component can specify which *type* of apartment it can live in, but it is up to COM to figure out at creation time exactly which apartment of that type the object will live in and which type of connection to the object, direct or marshaled, its creator will receive. To do this, COM+ considers the apartment to which the creating thread belongs. The matrix of outcomes is shown in Table 2-9. If an object is created in the same apartment as the thread that creates it, the thread gets a direct connection to the object, which is very fast. If the object is created in a different apartment, the thread gets a proxy/stub connection. When the thread makes a call to the proxy, it marshals the call into the apartment of the object. This call involves a thread switch, which is expensive in terms of performance. A *ThreadingModel* registry entry of *Single*, or no entry, represents a legacy case that I won't deal with.

> COM chooses an apartment for an object at creation time, based on the component's requirements and the creator's apartment.

To solve this performance problem of accessing objects in different apartments, COM+ provides us with a new type of apartment called the *neutral apartment* (NA), or sometimes, because geeks

> Objects living in the new "neutral" apartment never require a thread switch.

Table 2-9   Apartment in Which an Object Is Created

ThreadingModel Registry Entry	*Creating Thread in any STA of the Process*	*Creating Thread in the Process's Lone MTA*
Apartment	Creator's STA (direct)	Special-case STA (standard proxy)
Free	MTA (standard proxy)	MTA (direct)
Both	Creator's STA (direct)	MTA (direct)
Neutral	Neutral (lightweight proxy)	Neutral (lightweight proxy)

love their TLAs (three-letter acronyms; TLA itself is a TLA),[1] the *thread neutral apartment* (TNA). Unlike an STA or the MTA, the NA contains no threads, only objects (which is why I refer to it as the NA, to emphasize the fact that there's no T in it). An object with the registry entry *ThreadingModel=Neutral* is always created in the NA, regardless of the apartment occupied by the thread that creates it. The creating thread always receives a lightweight proxy.

When a thread makes a call to an NA object using this proxy, the call proceeds without changing threads, which makes it much faster than a standard thread-switching proxy call. This means that an object in the NA always receives its call on the thread of its caller, regardless of type. If an STA thread calls an NA object, the call is received on the STA thread. If an MTA thread calls an NA object, the call is received on the MTA thread. Any synchronization required by NA objects can be provided by the COM+ activities described in the next section.

Because objects that live in the NA can be accessed efficiently from both an STA or the MTA, I think that *Neutral* will eventually replace *Free* and *Both* as component types. Apart from legacy components that you don't want to rewrite, I can't think of any reason that you'd want to use the MTA. Objects that require thread affinity, especially those using windows for user interface work, will still need to live in an STA.

Synchronization

Allowing incoming calls only when an object is capable of handling them is a critical design requirement.

Anyone who has ever used a chain saw knows the hazards of being disturbed at the wrong moment. Similarly, an object can cause untold damage if an unruly thread joggles its elbow while the object performs delicate operations on a different thread. The

---

1. You can take this idea one step farther. I once read a message on a bulletin board describing what the author called an SDE, which stood for SDK Documentation Error. I immediately realized that I was in the presence of a new class of creature that I have named CCT, which stands for Clever Compound TLA. A CCT is a TLA in which one or more of the letters stands for another TLA. And of course CCT is itself a CCT.

previous section dealt with *which* thread was allowed to make a call into an object. The question of *when* a thread is allowed to make a call into an object is at least as critical.

Programming with multiple threads can make it easier to segregate a program's functionality logically, to schedule tasks, and to assign priorities, and it can also improve the efficiency with which resources are used. On the downside, robust multithreaded programming requires careful design and explicit use of defensive programming techniques to ensure that one thread doesn't cause damage by interfering with operations under the control of a different thread. These programming techniques are collectively called *synchronization*, or sometimes *serialization*.

Restricting calls in this manner is known as synchronization.

Writing correct synchronization code is difficult. It's hard to anticipate every possible concurrency situation, and bugs caused by wrong synchronization code are especially flaky and hard to reproduce. In classic COM, many component developers opted out of synchronization entirely by requiring their objects to reside only in STAs, discussed in the previous section. Only the single thread that occupies an STA is allowed to call methods on such an object. Calls that originate on other threads but that are directed to an STA object are routed by a proxy through the Windows message-queuing mechanism to ensure that they are actually received by the object only on the apartment's single thread. Since an individual object's methods will be called only from the single thread of the apartment in which it resides, the developer needs to write little or no synchronization code, and the component is therefore much easier to develop. See my article in the February 1997 *Microsoft Systems Journal* for more information on this model.

Writing correct synchronization code is difficult.

Unfortunately, the synchronization resulting from this architecture is purchased at the cost of thread affinity, which gets expensive when calls start going from one machine to another. Incoming calls from remote clients are received by threads in a system pool. A call destined for an object that lives in an STA must then be marshaled, via the Windows message-queuing mechanism, from the receiving thread to the thread that runs the STA in which the object resides. This takes time and CPU cycles that could be better used elsewhere, and is prone to bottlenecks if the receiving thread is busy.

The alternative is to write components that live in a process's lone NA, or previously the MTA. In this case, the incoming call could proceed directly to the object from the receiving thread. We wouldn't have to waste CPU cycles switching threads, we wouldn't have to worry about the receiving thread being busy, and we'd make the best use of multiple CPU chips on the server machine. The problem is that, because calls to an object can now come in on any thread at any time, component developers must write whatever synchronization code they need to make sure that their objects will still perform safely and correctly in the case of concurrent access. They essentially have to erect a temporary fence around themselves while making a cut with a chain saw and then take it down when they are finished.

COM+ provides activity-based synchronization services for developers who don't want to write their own.

Unfortunately, such synchronization code is extremely difficult to write, especially in the case of multiple machines. Fortunately, this problem is generic, so COM+ provides a generic solution called *activity-based synchronization*. An *activity* is a set of objects performing work on behalf of a single client, within which concurrent calls from multiple threads are not allowed. Think of an activity as a single logical thread that can span multiple processes and machines.

A component specifies the activity in which its objects must run.

Components that want to take advantage of activity-based synchronization are marked as such by using the Component Services snap-in, as shown in Figure 2-25. When a client thread creates an object, COM+ determines the activity in which to create the new object by consulting these administrative settings and the activity of the creator. The new object can wind up in the creator's activity (if any), in a new activity, or in no activity, as

Figure 2-25 *Setting a component's synchronization support.*

```
┌─────────────────────────────────────────────────┐
│ PingComponent.Pinger.1 Properties        [?][X] │
├─────────────────────────────────────────────────┤
│ General │ Transactions │ Security │ Activation │ Concurrency │ Advanced │
│                                                   │
│  ┌─ Synchronization support ──────────────────┐  │
│  │   ○ Disabled                               │  │
│  │   ○ Not Supported                          │  │
│  │   ○ Supported                              │  │
│  │   ◉ Required                               │  │
│  │   ○ Requires New                           │  │
│  └────────────────────────────────────────────┘  │
│                                                   │
│  ┌─ Threading Model ──────────────────────────┐  │
│  │   Single Thread Apartment                  │  │
│  └────────────────────────────────────────────┘  │
│                                                   │
│                                                   │
│  ┌────────────────────────────────────────────┐  │
│  │ ⓘ NOTE: Some synchronization options may be │  │
│  │   disabled due to the current transaction   │  │
│  │   or just in time activation settings.      │  │
│  └────────────────────────────────────────────┘  │
│                                                   │
│            [  OK  ] [ Cancel ] [ Apply ]          │
└─────────────────────────────────────────────────┘
```

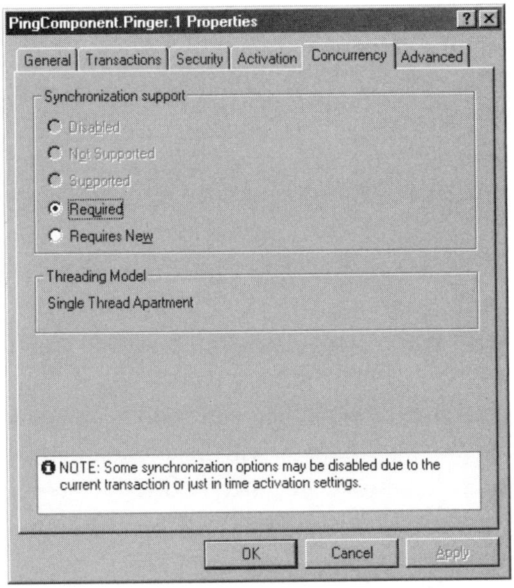

shown in Table 2-10. All transactional components must reside in an activity, otherwise one thread might be committing the transaction while another is trying to abort it. In addition, all STA components must reside in an activity, whether they are transacted or not.

Each activity contains a processwide synchronization lock. When a COM+ component makes a call into an activity other than its own, the proxy's interceptor attempts to acquire ownership of the lock. If the lock is currently free or is owned by the same activity as the caller, the call proceeds. If not, the caller waits until it can

A COM+ activity provides automatic synchronization services by waiting on, acquiring, and releasing a processwide lock.

Table 2-10   Activity in Which an Object Is Created

Synchronization Setting	Creator in an Activity	Creator NOT in an Activity
Not Supported	None	None
Supported	Creator's	None
Required	Creator's	New
Requires New	New	New

get ownership of the lock. If the owner of the lock does not release it by returning from the call that acquired the lock, the waiting call will fail with an error after a nonconfigurable system timeout interval, the duration of which is still being debated at the time of this writing. Once the caller acquires the lock, the call proceeds. When the call returns, the interceptor releases the lock. Incoming calls are processed in strictly first-in, first-out order; there is currently no way to use priority to jump to the head of the queue.

COM+'s activity-based synchronization properly handles the case of nested calls that span multiple machines. Suppose object A calls object B in a different activity on a different machine. Suppose that, within this call, object B makes a call back into object A. How does COM+ know that the incoming call is part of the same logical call stack and not a new incoming call from some random client? In the former case, the call should proceed immediately; in the latter case, the caller should be blocked until the first call completes. DCOM contains the notion of a *causality*, which you can think of as the logical ID of a stack of nested calls. It's a piece of data that accompanies a call, propagated by the proxy and stub. When a new call goes out from object A to object B, COM automatically generates a causality ID and attaches it to the call. When object B turns around and calls back into object A, COM+ checks the causality ID, determines that they are the same, and allows the call to proceed. If they had been different, indicating that they were not part of the same nested set of calls (part of the same causality), the incoming call would have been blocked instead.

There is one case in which the synchronization code doesn't work. Suppose you have two objects, A and B, in the same activity. Suppose you now have two client threads, T1 and T2. Suppose T1 calls a method on object A and T2 calls a method on object B. The first call to physically get through, let's say T1 for this example,

COM+ uses causality to properly identify nested calls even if they appear on different threads.

Here is the one place where COM+'s synchronization doesn't work and the way to avoid problems with it.

will acquire the lock. The second call, T2, will attempt to acquire the lock, but will be blocked because T1 already has it. It will stay blocked until T1 releases it, at which time T2 will be released and run. That's what you want, and that's what happens if the two threads are in the same process. The problem occurs if the two threads are in different processes. An activity lock is only process-wide, not machinewide. If T2 is in a different process from T1, the call will go through instead of being blocked, and you have the problems of concurrent access. To avoid this, clients should not share their objects, especially across process boundaries. If two different clients need to access the same piece of data, they should do it by creating two distinct object identities that access the same shared data state, as shown in Figure 2-26. Instead of a singleton object, consider using two separate objects that share a class static variable.

Clients should not share their objects, especially across process boundaries.

Figure 2-26 *Sharing state using two objects instead of sharing access to a singleton object.*

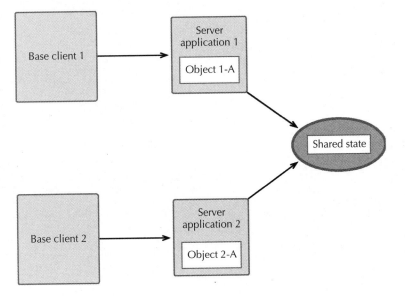

Chapter Three

Transactions

Business Problem Background

Maintaining the integrity of an enterprise system's data across multiple applications, users, and machines is an important and difficult task. The business logic of an electronic checking account application is extremely simple—you increment an account, you decrement an account, or you do one of each to make a payment. With a desktop application, it's pretty easy. However, when you scale that business logic to an enterprise application, new problems arise and you need new infrastructure to get the job done. This section presents some examples of the problems that arise in maintaining data integrity in an enterprise application.

Paying my phone bill requires the system to decrement the balance of my bank account and increment that of the phone company. Suppose that only one of those operations succeeds and the other fails. For example, suppose that decrementing my account succeeds, but the phone company's account is stuffed so full of money that incrementing it causes an arithmetic overflow error and crashes the incrementing object before it can write the new balance to disk. In this case, money would be destroyed (my money!)—taken from my account but never paid to my creditor. This would violate the integrity of the system's data, which we can't allow. We need to bind these operations together in such a manner that either both operations succeed together or both fail

> An enterprise application requires significant infrastructure to maintain the integrity of its data.

> Maintaining data integrity requires that the sub-operations comprising a larger operation either all succeed or all fail.

together. If they both succeed, fine; the phone company's got my money and I've got phone service for another month. If the credit to the phone company fails, the state of the system (in this case, my balance) needs to be rolled back to the state it was in before the operation started. My bill still hasn't been paid and I'll have to try again, but the data integrity of the system has not been violated.

Maintaining data integrity requires hiding intermediate states of operations from objects that shouldn't see them.

Since the bill-paying system is large and distributed, other bills are probably being paid and other housekeeping operations going on while my payment is taking place. Problems can arise when these other operations try to access information that my operation is currently using. Suppose an auditor application is checking the total of all accounts in the system and looks at both account balances in the middle of the transfer operation—after the deduction from my account but before the credit to the phone company's. The total amount of money in the system won't agree with its previous state. The auditor will think it sees the problem mentioned above, where one of the operations succeeded and the other failed, but its alarm will be false. The system would have been back in a legal state some small amount of time later, when the credit to the phone company's account was completed (or failed, and the initial debit to my account undone). But because the auditor looked into my operation at a bad time, the system appeared inconsistent. We need some means of keeping other operations from seeing the intermediate states of our operation before it finishes—a sort of dressing room in which the actor can change costumes unobserved before reappearing onstage.

Maintaining data integrity requires accounting for program or machine failure.

Finally, what happens if the operation requires two machines to coordinate the operation and one of them goes down? Suppose money is debited from my account on Machine A, the credit operation for the phone company's account begins on Machine B, and then some dimwit yanks machine B's plug out of the wall. Was the credit operation completed before the crash or was it not? Do we have to roll back the state of the first operation on

Machine A? How do we find out? This actually happened to me when using the Web site of the financial services company that handles my investment accounts. It took several hours on the phone to straighten out, and neither of us was happy about it. Writing the paper check would have been easier.

Solution Architecture

Now that we've seen some of the problems inherent in scaling relatively simple business logic to serve an enterprise, let's consider some solutions. We could write every component to handle every conceivable problem caused by every other component that it needed to work with. For example, we could write the debit and credit components to know about each other, and spend a lot of time and money developing code to specifically handle every conceivable failure scenario. This would be hideously expensive and take forever, we'd probably miss some weird combinations that we didn't think of, and the code wouldn't be reusable in other operations. Furthermore, this problem gets exponentially worse as more components and suboperations are added, as in the case of sending a confirmation message when the account transfers take place. Bad idea; got any others?

Writing every component to handle every conceivable problem caused by other components is seldom possible and never cost-effective.

A much better approach would be to have a generic manager that would oversee how these two components work together. Frank Zappa would call it the Central Scrutinizer, but we'll call it the DTC (distributed transaction coordinator) and each conglomerate operation a *transaction*. Each component within a transaction would do its own thing, in this case debit or credit an account, and then indicate to the DTC whether it was happy with the results. If all the participants were happy, the DTC would tell them to save all their changes (the new balances) and make the changes public, a process known as *committing* the transaction. If any one of them objected, the DTC would throw their changes away and

Read this whole paragraph.

restore the original state of the system (all the original bank balances), a process known as *aborting* the transaction. Thus only two outcomes of a transaction would be possible—complete success or total failure.

This approach is better than the previous example because the components are much, much easier to write—they don't have to know what any of the others are doing, just how to report to the DTC if they themselves are happy or sad. The DTC knows which other objects are participating in the transaction and coordinates the results among them. No one has to deal with intermediate failure states. Either everything works or nothing works.

The distributed transaction coordinator is a service that runs on Microsoft Windows 2000.

Where do we get this DTC? We could spend an awful lot of time and money writing one, or we could inherit a free one from the operating system. No prizes for getting the right answer here. Microsoft released their first DTC in Microsoft Transaction Server version 1, an add-on to Microsoft Windows NT that shipped in 1996. This release was a good first step, but it was a little tricky to use because it sat on top of COM instead of being integrated with it. The integration of MTS and COM is one of the main features of COM+. The COM+ run-time service performs almost all the negotiation with the DTC, so your objects don't have to do much.

A transaction workflow example begins here.

Simplest Transaction Example

The base client application starts the process by creating COM+ objects.

Let's look at the distributed transactional way of writing a bill payment application, the enterprise version of Quicken's business logic. The following example is based on the Sample Bank application that comes with COM+. It uses transactions to write a robust distributed bill-paying application. Geeks who like code can follow along in the sample source code found on this book's Web page.

The key point to keep in mind as you follow the example is that the author of the component doesn't have to do very much to inherit the transaction infrastructure from the operating system. In the following example, all the component author has to do is tell COM+ that the component requires a transaction and then signal the success or failure of the component's own operations that contribute to the transaction by calling *IObjectContext::Set-Complete* or *IObjectContext::SetAbort*. The rest of the complex dance is performed by the operating system.

The user interface for the sample application is shown in Figure 3-1. It is known as the "base client" application because it starts the ensuing stream of events.

Figure 3-1   *The Sample Bank application.*

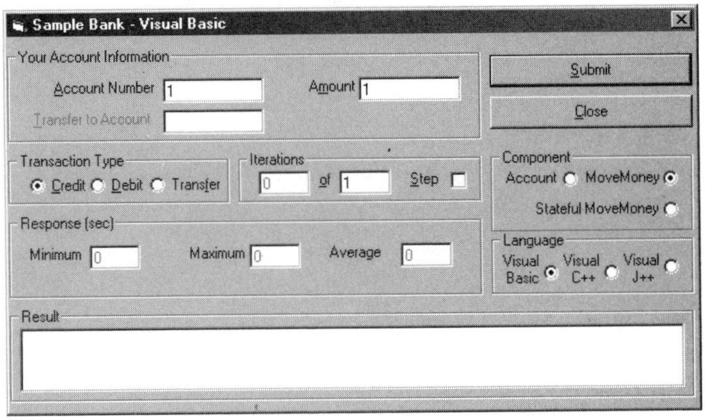

The user enters the dollar amount and then clicks the Submit button, as shown by (1) in Figure 3-2. In order to pay the bill, the base client application creates an instance of the *MoveMoney* component, using standard COM creation functions, in this case, the Visual Basic function *CreateObject* (2). The *MoveMoney* object will create and use other objects to credit one account and debit another.

The designer of the *MoveMoney* component decided that using transactions was the fastest, easiest way to get the job done safely. The designer therefore registered the *MoveMoney* component in the COM+ catalog as requiring a transaction. As discussed later in

When an object is created, COM+ uses the DTC to create a transaction for it, if needed.

this chapter, this step can be done either by the programmer when writing the component or by the administrator when registering the component, by using the Component Services snap-in. COM+ notices this attribute when it creates the *MoveMoney* object on behalf of the base client. "Aha!" says COM+. "This object needs a transaction and I don't have one yet." Where do all transactions originate? With the Central Scrutinizer, the DTC. So COM+ goes transparently to the DTC (through the *DtcGetTransactionManager* function) and asks it to create a new transaction (3). The DTC identifies each transaction internally with a 16-byte globally unique identifier (GUID), but for simplicity, I will call this transaction "T1." For its future use, COM+ stores a reference to T1 in the context of the *MoveMoney* object (4). Since transaction T1 was first created for its use, the *MoveMoney* object is said to be the *root* of transaction T1.

Figure 3-2   *The base client creates the object, and COM+ creates a transaction for the object.*

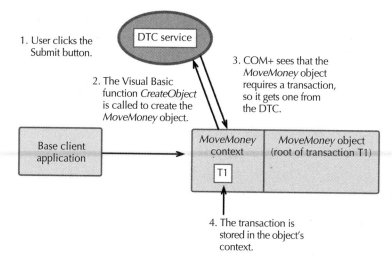

Our operation continues as shown in Figure 3-3. Having created the *MoveMoney* object, the base client now calls *MoveMoney's Perform* method (1).

The *MoveMoney* object then creates two new *Account* objects that I'll call *Account_A* and *Account_B*, one for my account and one for the phone company's (2). These objects perform the operation of incrementing or decrementing a single account. The *Account* component is also marked as requiring a transaction, just as the *MoveMoney* component was. When the *MoveMoney* object creates the new *Account* objects, COM+ notices by looking in *MoveMoney*'s context that *MoveMoney* is already a member of transaction T1. The new *Account* objects require transactions, but their creator already has one. Instead of creating a new transaction, COM+ copies the transaction information from the *Move-Money* object's context into the context of the new *Account* objects as well (3). We say that transaction T1 has been *propagated* to the new objects. Now all three objects, *MoveMoney*, *Account_A*, and *Account_B*, have a say in the outcome of T1. All three have to agree if the transaction is to be committed. Any one

When an object in a transaction creates other objects, COM+ can automatically propagate the existing transaction to the new objects.

Figure 3-3 *The transaction root object propagates the existing transaction to the objects that it creates.*

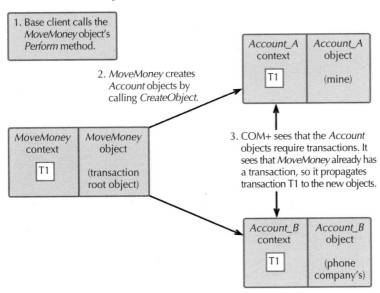

of the objects can veto the transaction and force the DTC to abort it. (Note that propagation of transactions is now handled automatically by COM+. Old MTS code that calls the *IObjectContext::CreateObject* method will still work, but this method is not needed in new code.)

The operation continues as shown in Figure 3-4. The *MoveMoney* object calls each *Account* object's *Post* method (1), telling the object to credit or debit an account. The *Account* objects, separately and knowing nothing of each other, open connections to SQL Server using ActiveX Data Objects (ADO)(2). SQL Server is a COM+ *resource manager* (RM), a piece of software that manages durable system state across COM+ transactions. An RM knows how to buffer changes to the resource that it manages (in this case, SQL tables) as the changes are made by the objects participating in a transaction, and then either publish them if the transaction commits or throw them away if the transaction aborts.

Figure 3-4 *The* MoveMoney *object calls the* Post *method on each* Account *object, and then the* Account *objects make SQL Server calls.*

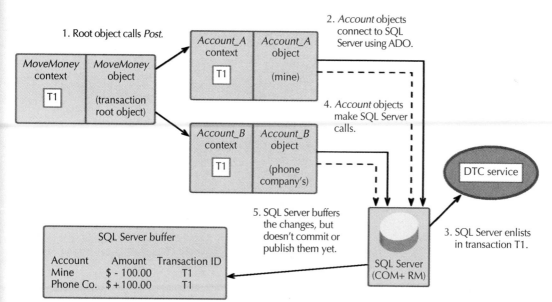

When the *Account* objects connect to SQL Server, the latter, being an RM, knows from looking at their contexts that *Account_A* and *Account_B* are both participating in transaction T1. SQL Server therefore *enlists* in transaction T1 by speaking to the DTC on its own machine (3). This figure shows SQL Server and the transaction root object running on the same machine. If they run on different machines, SQL Server's DTC will complete the enlistment by communicating with the DTC on the transaction root object's machine (not shown). The DTC now knows that SQL Server cares about the

When an object in a transaction uses a resource manager such as SQL Server, the RM enlists in the transaction by speaking to the DTC.

Commercially Available COM+ Resource Managers

Following is a list of RMs commercially available at the time of this writing. Most major commercial database applications have this capability. Microsoft Message Queue Server (MSMQ) does also, allowing message sending to be combined with database operations. Until very recently, writing an RM has been quite difficult, which is why more of them don't exist. COM+ now provides prefabricated infrastructure support for writing an RM, as discussed in the "Compensating Resource Managers" section later in this chapter. This infrastructure makes writing an RM significantly easier, so I would expect more RMs to be released soon.

- Microsoft SQL Server 6.5 and 7
- Microsoft Message Queue Server
- Oracle 7.3; Oracle 8 on Windows NT, Unix, and other platforms
- IBM DB2 on many IBM platforms including MVS, AS400, AIX, Windows NT, OS2
- Informix on Windows NT, Unix, and other platforms
- Sybase SQL Server on Windows NT, Unix, and other platforms
- CA Ingres on Windows NT, Unix, and other platforms

outcome of transaction T1, and will notify SQL Server when T1 commits or aborts so that SQL Server can commit or discard its changes. When the *Account* objects make SQL calls to credit or debit an account (4), SQL Server logs the changes internally (5). The changes to the account balances will not be copied from this buffer and made public until and unless transaction T1 commits.

Since the accounts taking part in the transaction are in a transitional state while the transaction is taking place, we need to be sure that no object not participating in the transaction can see or change their values. This is called *transactional isolation* and is discussed in more detail later in this chapter. It is the responsibility of the RM to provide whatever locking services it requires to ensure this isolation. In this case, SQL Server offers several different locking options that can be chosen by the database administrator.

An object calls *IObjectContext::SetComplete* to signal its satisfaction with a transaction.

Throughout this example, the *MoveMoney* and *Account* objects have been performing their business logic—for example, checking that enough money is in my account to cover the check that I've written. An object uses the *IObjectContext* interface to report to COM+ when it is finished with its work and whether it is satisfied with the results. An object obtains this interface by calling the *GetObjectContext* function, as discussed in Chapter 2. An object calls *IObjectContext::SetComplete* to signal that it has finished its work and that it is satisfied with the results. As far as the object is concerned, the transaction can commit. It calls *IObjectContext::SetAbort* to signal that it is finished but is not satisfied with the results and never will be, so the transaction *must* abort, no matter what any of the other objects think.

Transactions are generally short-lived.

A transaction is closed when the root object of the transaction is deactivated after returning from a call in which the object had indicated that it had finished its work. The objects in this example do this by calling *SetComplete* or *SetAbort*. A transaction is also closed if the root object of the transaction is released by the base client before it indicates that it is finished. A transaction also automatically aborts when an administratively set timeout interval (default = 60 seconds) expires. Transactions are generally designed to be short-lived, because the resource locks referred to in the previous paragraph can cause bottlenecks in the system. In this example, the transaction endures for only a single base-client method call. The case in which a transaction endures for a longer time is dealt with later in this chapter.

Our example continues as shown in Figure 3-5. Each *Account* object has called *SetComplete*, and so has the *MoveMoney* root object. COM+ looks at the status reported by all the objects in the transaction. In this example, all the objects are happy; none of them has vetoed the transaction by calling *IObjectContext::SetAbort*. They have given their *consent* to the transaction being committed, in the same way that wedding guests give their tacit approval of a marriage by remaining silent when the minister asks whether anyone objects.

If all objects are happy when the transaction closes, COM+ attempts to commit it.

Figure 3-5 *Happy objects calling* **IObjectContext::SetComplete.**

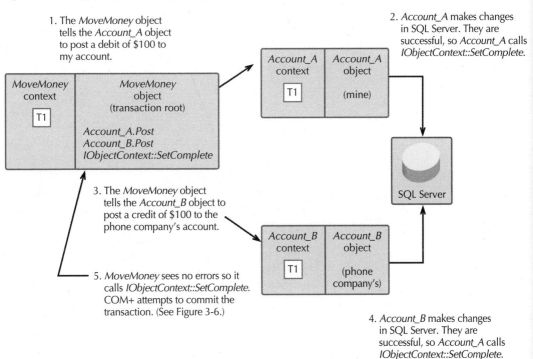

1. The *MoveMoney* object tells the *Account_A* object to post a debit of $100 to my account.

2. *Account_A* makes changes in SQL Server. They are successful, so *Account_A* calls *IObjectContext::SetComplete.*

3. The *MoveMoney* object tells the *Account_B* object to post a credit of $100 to the phone company's account.

5. *MoveMoney* sees no errors so it calls *IObjectContext::SetComplete.* COM+ attempts to commit the transaction. (See Figure 3-6.)

4. *Account_B* makes changes in SQL Server. They are successful, so *Account_A* calls *IObjectContext::SetComplete.*

Since all the objects have given their consent, COM+ now calls the DTC and attempts to commit the transaction, as shown by (1) in Figure 3-6. This process has two phases, *prepare* and *commit*. Don Box likens it to the exchange of wedding vows; just remember that the RMs are the parties making permanent commitments, not the objects.

Committing a transaction has two phases, prepare and commit.

In the prepare phase (2), the minister (DTC) asks each participant (each RM that has enlisted in the transaction) whether he or she is ready to do everything it takes to be married (commit the transaction, make it permanent). Commitment means different things to different people (Jimmy Carter, Bill Clinton) as it does to different RMs (SQL Server, MSMQ), but in the end they all come back and simply say "I do," or "I don't" (3). In the commit phase (4), the minister (DTC) pronounces the couple (all participating RMs; can get kinky) husband and wife (legal, durable, visible system state) (5).

Figure 3-6   *The two-phase transaction commit process.*

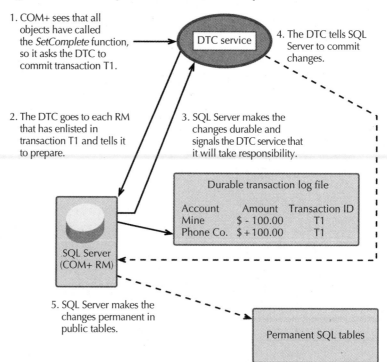

1. COM+ sees that all objects have called the *SetComplete* function, so it asks the DTC to commit transaction T1.

4. The DTC tells SQL Server to commit changes.

2. The DTC goes to each RM that has enlisted in transaction T1 and tells it to prepare.

3. SQL Server makes the changes durable and signals the DTC service that it will take responsibility.

5. SQL Server makes the changes permanent in public tables.

When the DTC tells it to prepare, the RM saves all of its state information in such a manner that failure to commit can no longer occur. It is up to the developer of the RM to decide what that means and to make it happen. If the RM returns successfully from the prepare phase, it is saying that it has accepted full responsibility for making the changes permanent. It's like depositing your paycheck at the ATM—you don't immediately see the change in your account, but incrementing your balance is now the bank's problem. You don't camp out on their doorstep to make sure the system did its job.

If the RM returns successfully from the prepare phase, it is saying that it has accepted full responsibility for making the changes permanent.

If all the RMs in the transaction signal that they have successfully completed the prepare phase, the transaction can no longer fail. The DTC tells the RMs to commit the transaction. If an RM crashes after successfully completing the prepare phase but before receiving the commit notification, it will query the DTC when it starts up again to find out whether the transaction it had prepared should be committed or aborted. It doesn't matter whether the groom passes out after saying "I do": the first thing he'll do after someone throws cold water on him is ask the minister, "Well, did she or didn't she?" If the bride also said, "I do," he's still hooked. Now you see one of the reasons that RMs are hard to write.

If an RM does not respond to the prepare instruction within a specified timeout interval (the groom ditches the bride at the altar), or responds with an error code that it was unable to prepare (the bride says "I don't"), the DTC tells all RMs to abort the transaction (the minister tells the couple to go home). The RMs then throw away their buffered changes (return the wedding dress and rented tux, tear up the marriage license, give back the rings), leaving the system in its original (unmarried) state.

If an RM does not respond to the prepare instruction within a specified timeout interval, or responds with an error code that it was unable to prepare, the DTC tells all RMs to abort the transaction.

Note that the transactional objects do not participate in the two-phase commit process, only the enlisted RMs do. The objects gave their consent to the marriage when they called *SetComplete* before the commit and are not consulted again. It is the RMs who actually modify the system state. In fact, the objects never do find out from COM+ what the final state of the transaction was.

If any object is unhappy
with the results of the
transaction, COM+ uses
the DTC to abort it.

Suppose, however, that not every object was happy. Suppose that
the phone company's *Account* object was unable to increment the
balance. Instead of *SetComplete*, that object might have called
SetAbort, as shown in Figure 3-7. In this case, when the transaction closes, COM+ calls the DTC and tells it to abort the transaction. The DTC then goes to each RM that has enlisted in the
transaction and tells it to throw away its changes and clean up.
The minister doesn't even ask the couple if they do or they don't.
At least one of the wedding guests has informed the minister that
the couple has flunked the blood test. Everyone goes home.

In Figure 3-7, *Account_B*'s operation failed, and both *Account_B*
and *MoveMoney* called *IObjectContext::SetAbort*. Any one of
these events would be sufficient to abort the transaction. Even if

Figure 3-7 *An unhappy object aborts the transaction by calling* **IObjectContext::SetAbort.**

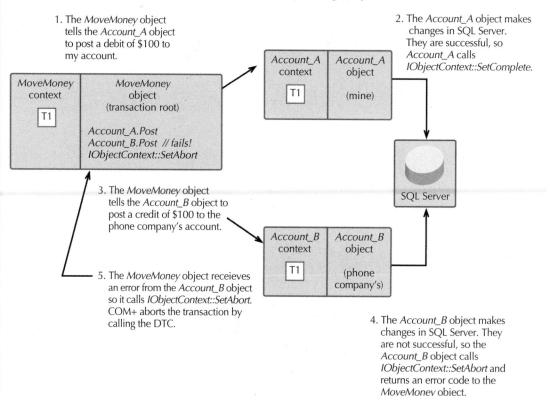

1. The *MoveMoney* object tells the *Account_A* object to post a debit of $100 to my account.

2. The *Account_A* object makes changes in SQL Server. They are successful, so *Account_A* calls *IObjectContext::SetComplete.*

3. The *MoveMoney* object tells the *Account_B* object to post a credit of $100 to the phone company's account.

5. The *MoveMoney* object receieves an error from the *Account_B* object so it calls *IObjectContext::SetAbort.* COM+ aborts the transaction by calling the DTC.

4. The *Account_B* object makes changes in SQL Server. They are not successful, so the *Account_B* object calls *IObjectContext::SetAbort* and returns an error code to the *MoveMoney* object.

MoveMoney had called *SetComplete*, *Account_B*'s call to *SetAbort* would have aborted the transaction. The designer of the *Account* component will probably return an error code to *MoveMoney* after calling *SetAbort* so that *MoveMoney*'s business logic will know that the transaction is doomed and not waste time doing more work on it. *MoveMoney* will probably also want to pass an informative error code to the base client so that the user knows where the problem lies and whom to contact to correct it. You have to write this error-handling code, but the committing or aborting of the transaction and the saving or discarding of the database changes is handled transparently by the DTC and the RMs.

Properties of Transactions

The term *transaction* is highly overloaded. That's geekspeak for having many different meanings. Jim Gray of Microsoft Research, in his foreword to Bernstein and Newcomer's *Principles of Transaction Processing* (Morgan Kaufman, 1997), refers to transactions as "the contract law of distributed systems." For the purposes of this book, *transaction* will have two meanings: first, just a simple generic unit of work that complies with the ACID properties discussed below; and second, the Microsoft software implementation that provides these useful units of work to the world.

A transaction should be able to pass the ACID test.

We like to say that a transaction is a unit of work that passes the ACID test, where ACID stands for atomicity, consistency, isolation, and durability. It's a cool acronym, but what the heck does it really mean?

Atomicity means that all the operations within the transaction either succeed or fail as a unit. Either the money leaves my account *and also* arrives in the phone company's, or neither operation happens. Atomicity means that neither the client application nor any of the objects have to deal with intermediate failure states— either all the changes worked or none of them did. Every object that participates in the transaction can cause it to abort and roll back the state of the world to the values it had before the transaction

A is for *atomicity*.

started. When an object goes to increment the phone company's account and fails, it aborts the transaction. It doesn't know what other objects, if any, that transaction contains or whether they succeeded or failed. The object is saying "Hey, I can't get it done. I don't know or care who else is taking part in this transaction or what they've done—we all need to go back to the way we were before. Make it so, eventually, please."

C is for *consistency*, which really means legality.

Consistency is a somewhat misleading term. It seems to want a preposition—consistent *with* something. The pioneers of transaction processing just might have fudged this one a bit in order to get a catchy acronym. I find it easier to understand if I think of consistency as really meaning legality. In this sense, consistency means that all the resources that participate in a transaction are left in a legal state at the end of the transaction, regardless of whether it commits or aborts. This makes the client's programming job easier because the client can safely make the assumption that the state is consistent when it starts and when it finishes. The system can and usually does pass through inconsistent states *during* the transaction; you just can't leave it in an inconsistent state at the end. An RM must be able to attain the state that defines consistency (legality) for itself, or it has to abort the transaction to return itself (and all the other RMs) to its previous consistent state. For example, every entry in a relational database must have its own unique primary key—if an entry doesn't, the database is not consistent (its state is not legal). If the database manager runs out of primary key numbers, it won't be able to attain consistency after trying to add a new record, so it will abort the transaction.

Consistency means that when a transaction is over, it's over. Whether the transaction was committed or aborted, all the participants have cleaned up their workshops and put their tools away so nothing is left for anyone to trip over. Norm Abrams (the master carpenter on the TV show *This Old House*) never did finish building his own house after three years, probably because he worked and traveled too much. His wife lost her patience (the transaction timed out) and her temper, but Norm couldn't get back to a consistent state, neither committing (finishing) nor aborting (bulldozing) the house. Because he couldn't achieve a consistent state, he wound up instead with a violation of system integrity (a divorce).

Isolation means that no one outside a transaction can see the intermediate results of that transaction while it is in progress. In the auditing example at the beginning of this chapter, because the intermediate state of a payment operation was not isolated from the auditing application, the latter thought it saw illegal combinations of balances, an inconsistent state. It's OK for the state to be inconsistent during a transaction; you just can't let anyone outside the transaction see it while it is. For example, database RMs will lock the records being used in a transaction so that they can't be viewed by anyone not participating in that transaction. Another example: I didn't want the public to see this book before it had been edited because it was full of errors (in an inconsistent state, and don't touch that line). I put it in a private directory on my Web server and gave the password to only the geeks who were proofreading or tech-editing it (participating in the transaction). That's isolation. The objects within the transaction work together, but their work is invisible to any outside agency. Atomicity means that you can't split the functionality of the objects (the particles within the atom), and isolation means that you can't even look at them.

I is for *isolation.*

While part of the classic transaction properties, isolation is sometimes sacrificed for easier component development and a better match of component function to business process. This is discussed in the "Compensating Transactions" section later in this chapter.

D is for durability. When the money moves from my account on one machine to the phone company's on another machine, it's not enough for each machine to keep the new account balances in volatile RAM. What if the power fails? The new system state—the new account balances—will be lost. Worse, what if the power fails on one machine but not on the other? One part of the system state will be lost and the other won't, which is an inconsistent (illegal) situation. The final property of a transaction is that the new, consistent system state has to be written to a medium that will survive a system failure, such as a log file or a database record, and flushed to disk. That's *durability*. Atomicity means that the operations all succeeded or failed together, and durability means that the results of that success or failure stay together even if part of the system fails.

The degree of durability required varies from one system to another. The most basic form of durability is protection against a system software crash or power failure. This means getting the new consistent state out of volatile silicon and onto nonvolatile iron. But does durability of transactions mean that the system state will survive a malicious computer virus? A fire in the computer room? The sun going supernova? In this sense, durability means as much durability as you want to pay for.

Specifying a Component's Use of Transactions

The author of each component specifies whether the component requires a transaction and how it deals with transactions it encounters in its journeys. The mechanisms used to create this specification are shown in Figures 3-8, 3-9, and 3-10. The Component Services snap-in provides a user interface (UI) for specifying the transaction properties of a component, as shown in Figure 3-8.

Figure 3-8 *Using the Component Services snap-in to specify the transaction attribute of a component.*

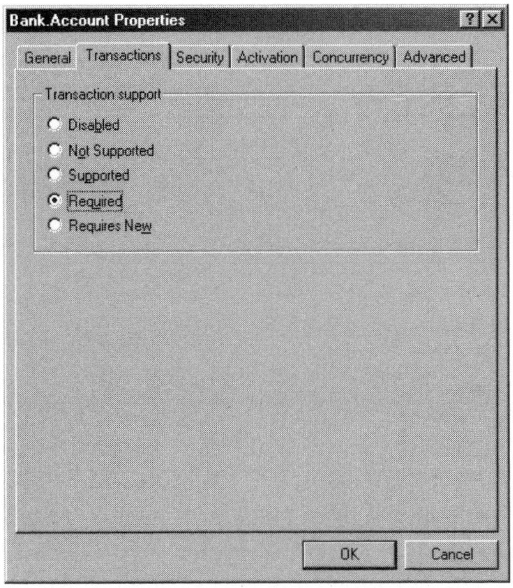

C++ programmers using Interface Definition Language (IDL) can specify transactional attributes by using IDL directives, as shown in Figure 3-9.

These directives cause the transactional attribute to be contained in the component's type library. High-level tools such as Visual Basic or Visual J++ generally bypass IDL and write their type

The developer of each component specifies that component's use of transactions.

Figure 3-9 *Using IDL to specify the transaction attribute of an object.*

```
[
    uuid(04CF0B76-1989-11D0-B917-0080C7394688),
    helpstring("Account Class"),
    TRANSACTION_REQUIRED
]
coclass CAccount
{
    [default] interface IAccount;
};
```

libraries directly into their component files. These tools will generally provide a user interface to allow the programmer to make a choice, as shown in Figure 3-10.

Figure 3-10 *Using Visual Basic to specify the transaction attribute of an object.*

All the components in the Sample Bank application use the same attribute, which is *Requires Transaction.* This is one of five transactional attributes from which a programmer can choose. These attributes and their effect on transaction creation and propagation are described in the following list and illustrated in Figure 3-11 (on page 90).

A component can require the absence of a transaction.

1. *Does Not Support Transactions:* Component *A* requires the absence of a transaction. It does not support transactions at all and doesn't want to be around any. If the object is created within the context of an existing transaction (that is to say, by an object that is already part of a transaction), the transaction is not propagated to the new nonsupporting object nor to any downstream objects that it might create. A better name for this attribute would be "swallows transactions." Choosing this attribute limits the use of your component: you can't place it between one transactional component and another, as it will not pass the transaction downstream. Even if your component doesn't use transactions itself, you'll probably find it more useful if you don't forbid the propagation of other components' transactions. Make sure this attribute is what you want before you choose it.

2. *Supports Transactions:* Component *B* is indifferent to the presence or absence of a transaction. If the object is created within the context of an existing transaction, the transaction is propagated to the new object and to any downstream objects that it might create. If it is created outside the context of a transaction, no new transaction is created. This attribute is generally used when your component doesn't need a transaction for its own work but wants to be able to work with components that do. A better name for this property would be "works and plays well with others."

3. *Requires Transaction:* Component *C* must have a transaction in order to do its work. If the object is created outside the context of a transaction, COM+ uses the DTC to create a new transaction. If the object is created within the context of an existing transaction, that transaction is propagated to the new object. The *MoveMoney* and *Account* components used in the example earlier in this chapter have this attribute.

4. *Requires New Transaction:* The component must always be the root of a new transaction. Whether or not the object is created within the context of a transaction, COM+ always goes to the DTC and creates a new transaction with this object at the root. For example, an auditing object with several transactional objects downstream of it might want the different segments of its audit to succeed or fail atomically together but not affect the outcome of the operation it was auditing.

5. *Disabled:* The component wants nothing to do with automatic transaction management in COM+. It will do whatever it wants to do with transactions by communicating directly with the DTC. This attribute is used by hardcore geeks for programming nonstandard behavior.

Figure 3-11 *Downstream propagation of a transaction according to the attributes of its components (the Disabled attribute is not shown).*

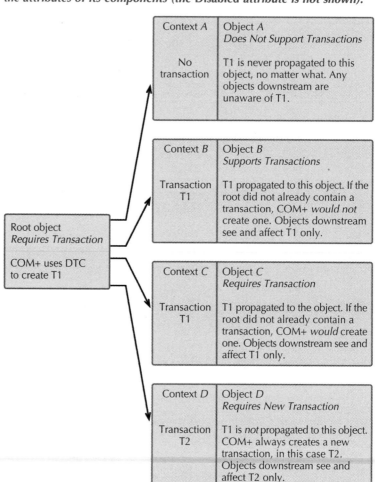

Context A	Object A *Does Not Support Transactions*
No transaction	T1 is never propagated to this object, no matter what. Any objects downstream are unaware of T1.

Context B	Object B *Supports Transactions*
Transaction T1	T1 propagated to this object. If the root did not already contain a transaction, COM+ *would not* create one. Objects downstream see and affect T1 only.

Root object
Requires Transaction

COM+ uses DTC
to create T1

Context C	Object C *Requires Transaction*
Transaction T1	T1 propagated to the object. If the root did not already contain a transaction, COM+ *would* create one. Objects downstream see and affect T1 only.

Context D	Object D *Requires New Transaction*
Transaction T2	T1 is *not* propagated to this object. COM+ always creates a new transaction, in this case T2. Objects downstream see and affect T2 only.

Committing or Aborting Transactions

The transaction-vote bit indicates whether the object currently allows its transaction to commit.

Each object's context contains two bits that are important when it participates in transactions. One bit indicates whether an object would currently allow the transaction to which it belongs to commit. I've seen this called the "consistent" or the "happy" bit, but I think its function is clearest if we call it the *transaction-vote* bit.

An object that sets this bit is saying, "It's OK by me if the transaction commits now. I am in a consistent (legal) state." An application that clears this bit is saying the opposite.

An object can change its transaction vote at any time until it is deactivated. At that point, the object's transaction vote becomes irrevocable. When it closes a transaction, COM+ checks the state of this bit in the context of every object within the transaction to determine whether the transaction can be committed or must be aborted. Remember, even a single objection causes a transaction to abort. If your object is deactivated with its transaction-vote bit in the abort state, that entire transaction is doomed, no matter what any other object in the transaction does. The transaction hasn't stopped breathing yet, but it is nonnegotiably dead and unrevivable.

The second bit controls the object's lifetime. It's often called the "done" bit, but its functionality is most clearly illustrated if we call it the *deactivate-on-return* bit. An object that sets this bit is saying that it has finished its work, that it has done everything it had to do. COM+ checks the state of this bit after the return of each method call on an object. If the bit is on, COM+ will deactivate the object if the component is using just-in-time (JIT) activation, discussed later in this chapter. All transactional objects must use JIT activation; nontransactional objects can do so if they desire. COM+ either releases the object or returns it to the pool if pooling is enabled for that object. If the object is the root of a transaction (as was *MoveMoney* in the previous example), COM+ will close the transaction, checking the transaction-vote bit of all the objects and committing or aborting accordingly.

When a transaction root object method returns with the deactivate-on-return bit set, COM+ closes the transaction.

When an object method returns with the deactivate-on-return bit set, COM+ deactivates the object.

An object can manipulate these two bits by using the *IObjectContext* interface shown in Table 3-1. The original interface of MTS, it contains four methods that set the state of both these bits simultaneously. You can also set each bit individually by using the *IContextState* interface, whose methods are shown in Table 3-2.

COM+ checks the deactivate-on-return bit when an object method call returns.

This interface is new to COM+. It is obtained through the *CoGet-ObjectContext* function or by querying the *IObjectContext* interface.

SetComplete means "I'm happy and I'm done."

SetAbort means "I'm done, but I'm not happy."

I discussed the *IObjectContext::SetComplete* and *IObject-Context::SetAbort* methods in the Sample Bank application earlier. The object that calls them is finished with its work, and is either happy or unhappy with the results, as indicated by which of these respective methods it has called. Since both methods set the deactivate-on-return bit, they tell COM+ to deactivate the object on return from the method call.

Table 3-1 *IObjectContext* Interface Methods That Affect the Transaction-Vote and Deactivate-on-Return Bits of a Transaction

Method	Transaction Vote	Deactivate on Return
SetComplete	Commit	Yes
SetAbort	Abort	Yes
EnableCommit (default transaction state)	Commit	No
DisableCommit	Abort	No

Table 3-2 The *IContextState* Interface Methods

Method	Description
SetDeactivateOnReturn	Turns on or off the bit indicating whether the object wants COM+ to deactivate it when it returns from the current method.
GetDeactivateOnReturn	Gets current status of the bit indicating whether the object wants COM+ to deactivate it when it returns from the current method.
SetMyTransactionVote	Turns on or off the bit indicating whether the object would veto its transaction committing at the current time.
GetMyTransactionVote	Gets current status of the bit indicating whether the object would veto its transaction committing at the current time.

The *EnableCommit* and *DisableCommit* methods are a little harder to understand. Since they do not set the deactivate-on-return bit, they are used when an object's functionality needs to span more than one method call, which the Sample Bank application does not demonstrate. An object that calls *DisableCommit* clears both the transaction-vote and the deactivate-on-return bits, indicating that it is currently in an inconsistent state, unhappy with the world, but that it has not yet finished its work. Since COM+ does not deactivate it, the object might become happy at some future time. The object is saying, "If you need my answer right now on the transaction, the answer is no. Maybe later, after I've done some more work in response to other function calls, I can agree to commit the transaction, but right now I can't."

DisableCommit means "I'm not happy, but I'm not done either."

An object that calls *EnableCommit* is saying that it is currently in a consistent state, happy with the world, would vote to commit the transaction, but doesn't want to be deactivated. It wants to stay around to potentially service more calls. The object is saying, "I'm happy, but I'm not necessarily done. I can take another method call if you think I have something constructive to offer you, but I don't need to have one. Of course, that other method call might make me unhappy and force me to abort the transaction, but that's showbiz."

EnableCommit means "I'm happy, but I don't have to be deactivated now."

The default state of the transaction bits when an object is first activated is *EnableCommit*—the transaction-vote bit is voting to commit, and the deactivate-on-return bit is turned off. You can, if you like, change the default state of the latter bit on a per-method basis by marking a method as Auto-Done. The user interface for doing this is shown in Figure 3-12.

In this case, the deactivate-on-return bit will be set when you enter a method. If an object method returns successfully (return code *S_OK* in C++, not throwing an error in VB or Java), COM+ considers it equivalent to calling *IObjectContext::SetComplete*. The transaction-vote bit is set to commit, and the object is deactivated. If a method returns unsuccessfully (*HRESULT* with high bit

Objects that mark themselves as Auto-Done in the catalog can indicate their outcomes simply by returning success or failure codes.

Figure 3-12   *The user interface for marking a method Auto-Done.*

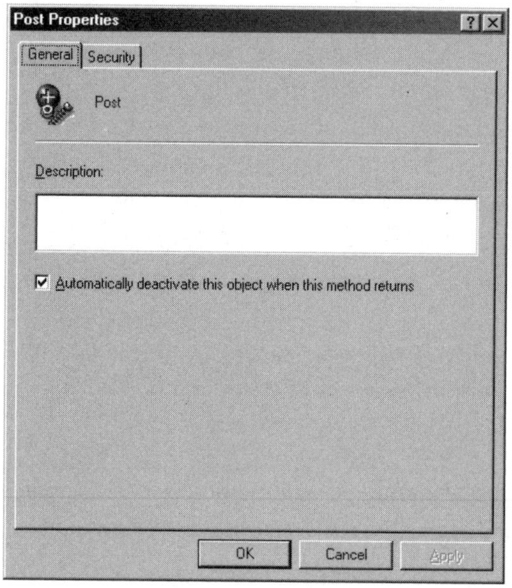

set in C++, throwing an error in Visual Basic or Java), COM+ considers it equivalent to setting *IObjectContext::SetAbort*. The transaction-vote bit is set to abort, and the object is deactivated. Making explicit calls to any of the state management interfaces within the method will override the Auto-Done settings. If the *Account* object had marked its *Post* method as Auto-Done, it would not have needed to call *IObjectContext::SetComplete* or *SetAbort*. It could simply have returned *S_OK* or *E_FAIL*.

Just-In-Time Activation in Transactions

JIT activation is a mechanism provided by the operating system whereby actual instances of an object are activated just prior to the first call made to them and are deactivated immediately after they finish their work.

Just-in-time (JIT) activation is a mechanism provided by the operating system whereby actual instances of an object are activated just prior to the first call made to them and are deactivated immediately after they finish their work. When I say that an object is *activated*, I mean that it is either created or fetched from a pool of existing objects. When I say that an object is *deactivated*, I mean that it is either destroyed or placed back in the pool. (Object pooling is discussed later in the "Transactions and Object

State" section of this chapter.) Use of JIT activation is mandatory for transactional components. Nontransactional components can also use it if needed.

In JIT activation, the client creates an object and receives a standard proxy and stub connected by a channel, as shown in Figure 3-13.

Figure 3-13 *Just-in-time activation: the client creates an object as usual.*

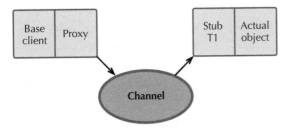

Once the object is created, the client makes calls to it as usual. When the object is deactivated, COM+ releases its reference to the actual server-side object, as shown in Figure 3-14, and the object is destroyed or placed back in the pool.

Figure 3-14 *Just-in-time activation causes the stub to release the object when the transaction ends.*

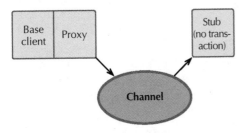

However, since the client has not released its reference to the object, the client-side proxy still exists, and so do the server-side stub and the channel connecting them, as shown in the diagram. When the client next makes a call to the proxy, the proxy communicates with the stub via the channel, and a new instance of the desired object is activated "just in time," as shown in Figure 3-15.

JIT activation activates and deactivates objects as they are needed on the server, without the client's knowledge.

Figure 3-15 *A client making a call on the proxy causes the stub to activate an object just in time for the client's use.*

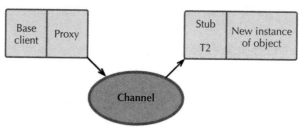

JIT was originally presented as a solution to the resource-loading problems caused by clients hogging resources.

JIT activation was first presented to the world as a scalability feature for recovering resources. A user-driven client application often creates an object, makes a method call, and holds on to the object for later use. Five minutes or an hour later, the client might make another method call. In between, the object is hanging around, tying up resources. This doesn't matter much in the desktop environment, where you typically have one, two, or three clients per COM server, but an enterprise server can easily have a hundred or more clients coming and going. You can see the resource-loading problems that would arise if the clients all hung on to resources that they weren't currently using, because they might need them later. A perfect example of this kind of problem happened when America Online switched to flat-rate pricing. Everyone started spending more time online, so an open line got harder to find. Since an open line was harder to find, users didn't hang up once they got one. It took AOL quite a while and many frustrated customers before they installed enough modems to handle the load.

JIT activation might not recover many resources.

JIT activation results in a certain amount of resource reclamation, but often less than you think. When a transaction is completed, its server-side objects are deactivated and their resources released. However, even though the actual COM object is deactivated, the channel and stub stay in place. Exact measurements will have to await the final release of COM+, but in MTS version 2, these used about 1 KB of RAM. So only if your object is taking up more space than these infrastructural items will JIT activation provide much profit in terms of sheer number of bytes. JIT activation makes you more of a profit when deactivating an object recovers a scarce, expensive resource, such as a database connection.

The real advantage of JIT activation, particularly when combined with object pooling, is that it enforces transactional correctness, specifically consistency and isolation, with the greatest possible speed. The key point here, new to nontransactional programmers, is that once a transaction is complete, objects are not allowed to retain any information resulting from the transaction, because the information might be inaccurate. Why is this?

The major advantage of JIT activation is that it enforces transactional correctness while still maximizing speed.

Remember that the objects participating in a transaction are not notified of the outcome. The *Account* object representing my account in the sample detailed earlier doesn't know whether the credit to the phone company's account succeeded or failed. It is the resource managers, in this case SQL Server, that know the outcome of the transactions and modify the account balances accordingly. The objects trust the DTC and the RMs to make the right outcome happen based on the votes of the objects.

Suppose that my *Account* object stored the new balance of my account, minus the payment to the phone company, in an instance variable. Suppose the transaction then aborted because the phone company's account couldn't be incremented. My account balance would be rolled back in the underlying data store, but the *Account* object would contain an incorrect cached copy. The object's state would be illegal, inconsistent. We can't allow this to happen.

Transactional components must not retain information about the transaction after it closes.

Without JIT activation, we would have to explicitly write our transactional components so that they would not accept an incoming call after completing their transactional work, thereby forcing the client to release them and re-create them. This would require programming effort on the part of both component and client developers. In addition, tearing down the proxy, stub, and channel every time would be hideously inefficient. JIT activation

JIT activation forces you to think about your object's state.

ensures that any leftover information in an object is dumped when the transaction closes, thereby prohibiting objects from stepping on their own toes by applying nontransactional mindsets to the new transactional world they've entered. And because only the object is deactivated and the infrastructure relating to that object stays in place, the operation happens as quickly as possible.

Transactions and Object State

Lots of noise gets made over "statelessness" in COM+.

Much fuss is made in the literature over "statefulness vs. statelessness" in transactional components. I have no "one true way" revelation to offer you here, only tools you can use, each with advantages and disadvantages. Which would I use? The one that makes me the most money.

COM is silent on the issue of where an object's state lives.

Most programmers think of their object's instance data (member variables in C++, public variables in Visual Basic) as their object's "state." Instance data does get dumped when an object is deactivated, leading some people to refer to objects of this type as "stateless." But COM speaks only of interfaces, never of state. COM is silent on the issue of where an object's state can or can't, must or mustn't, live. Your object's immediate client, COM+, is employing your object in a way you haven't seen before. To take advantage of that client, which you would very much like to do, you have to reconsider the assumptions about state that you've unconsciously held but probably never stated (groan).

COM objects have always stored their state in a variety of locations.

COM objects have always stored their state in many different places. For example, embedded spreadsheet objects store their state in persistent streams inside a document file. Their behavior lives in one place, the server application, and their state in another. The object reads its state from the document file when the object is activated and stores it back when it's deactivated. I've had customers choose an .EXE server over a .DLL server so they could share singleton object state between one client application and another client application by using global variables inside the .EXE. I've had other customers solve the same problem using a .DLL server and a shared memory file map. Other COM objects might depend solely on their clients to keep track of their state—

think of an HTML page containing an ActiveX control. Properties of the control, such as its background color and font, will often be encoded in the HTML page and fed to the control by the browser. Object state has always lived all over the place; you've just never really thought of it before.

In his ActiveX/COM column in the March 1998 issue of *Microsoft Systems Journal,* Don Box identified four locations in which an object's state could live. These areas are summarized in Table 3-3.

First, an object's state can be stored in the client application. This is the strategy used by the *Account* object in the earlier sample. Its *Post* method requires the client to supply the account number and the amount of money in question as parameters to every function call. The object does not retain any state information in instance variables from one call to another. Every piece of state that it needs at any given time has to be supplied by the client.

An object can store its state in the client application.

Next, an object can store its state in its own instance variables. This is a good location for volatile information (information that exists only during the lifetime of a transaction) that does not need to be shared with other objects. The *Account* component does not use this mechanism for anything, because it does all of its work in a single function call. An example of information that could live at this level would be the intermediate results of calculations for objects whose lifetimes spanned more than one method call.

An object can store its volatile state in its own instance variables.

Table 3-3   Possible Locations for State of a COM+ Object

Location of State	Lifetime of State	Speed of Access	Ease of Programming
Client	Varies, but not the object's problem	Varies, but not the object's problem	Harder for the client, easier for the object
Component instance data	Same as object	Fastest	Easiest
Resource dispenser (shared property manager or pooled object)	Varies from transaction lifetime to application lifetime	Medium	Not bad
Resource manager (database)	Persistent	Slowest	Hardest

An object might want to store its volatile state in such a way that it can be shared with other objects. COM+ provides mechanisms for doing this, such as resource dispensers and object pooling. The ODBC connection manager is a resource dispenser. When the first *Account* object requested a database connection, the ODBC connection manager created a new one. When the first *Account* object released it, the ODBC connection manager didn't destroy the connection, but instead placed it in an internal pool. When the second *Account* object requested a database connection, the ODBC connection manager noticed that it referred to the same database as the first *Account* object and thus reused the first connection from its pool instead of creating a new one. You didn't notice any of this happening, as it was handled transparently by the ODBC connection manager. In addition to the ODBC connection manager, COM+ also provides the shared property manager, a resource dispenser used for sharing individual data values between objects.

An object can share its volatile state with other objects through resource dispensers or object pooling.

The new object-pooling feature of COM+ makes it relatively easy to share state between objects in a transaction and is described in full in the following section. Using object pooling is much easier than writing a resource dispenser, so I would expect to see this feature used more often in the future.

An object can use resource managers to safely manage its persistent state.

Finally, an object can use a resource manager, such as SQL Server, to safely manage its persistent state. In the Sample Bank application, the bank account balances of the various depositors was the state that the objects modified.

But wait a minute. Isn't the combination of state and behavior what we mean by the word "object?" Doesn't separating the two mean that we aren't programming objects any more, and isn't programming with objects a Good Thing? Don't bother me with religious semantics, I've got a product to ship. And so do you, so stop wasting time arguing about how many pinheads can dance on an angel and get to work. To get it done, we both have to carefully think about where our object's state should be located at any given time.

Transactions and Object Pooling

JIT activation means that objects in a COM+ server are created and destroyed frequently. To save CPU cycles, we would like some way to release an object's resources without actually destroying the object and then reinitialize its virgin state and use it again without having to create it. It's the oldest trade-off in all of computing: space for speed. Object pooling combined with JIT activation is the way to obtain maximum speed from COM+.

Object pooling combined with JIT activation is the way to obtain maximum speed from COM+.

The concept is quite simple. Using the Component Services snap-in, shown in Figure 3-16, the administrator marks a component as pooled. When the COM+ application containing the component is first activated, COM+ creates the number of objects specified as the minimum pool size and holds them in a pool. When a client creates an object, through either a direct request or a JIT function call, COM+ first checks the pool to see whether an object of the specified type is available. If so, COM+ will activate the object from the pool instead of creating a new one. If not, COM+ will create a new one, up to the maximum specified size of the pool.

An object needs a way to know when it is being activated or deactivated so it can initialize its virgin state or release its resources. The object receives these notifications by implementing the *IObjectControl* interface, whose methods are shown in Table 3-4.

When an object is activated, COM+ queries for the *IObjectControl* interface and calls its *Activate* method. This is the object's chance to do whatever initialization it needs to make itself ready to deal

Figure 3-16 *Using the Component Services snap-in to enable object pooling.*

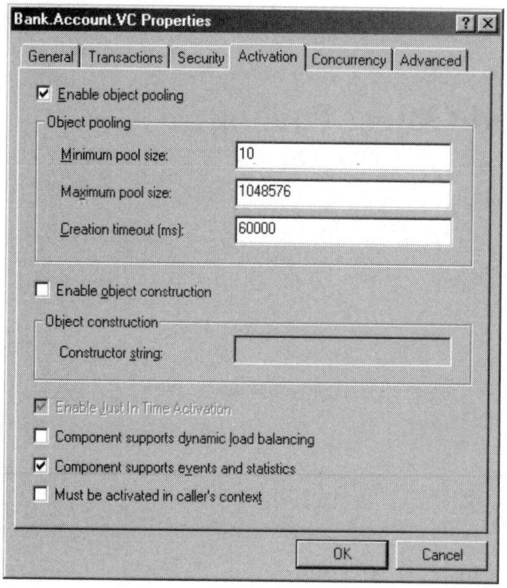

```
Bank.Account.VC Properties                                    ? X

 General | Transactions | Security | Activation | Concurrency | Advanced |

   ☑ Enable object pooling
    ┌ Object pooling ─────────────────────────────────────────┐
    │                                                          │
    │   Minimum pool size:        10                           │
    │                                                          │
    │   Maximum pool size:        1048576                      │
    │                                                          │
    │   Creation timeout (ms):    60000                        │
    │                                                          │
    └──────────────────────────────────────────────────────────┘

   ☐ Enable object construction
    ┌ Object construction ────────────────────────────────────┐
    │   Constructor string:                                    │
    └──────────────────────────────────────────────────────────┘

   ☑ Enable Just In Time Activation
   ☐ Component supports dynamic load balancing
   ☑ Component supports events and statistics
   ☐ Must be activated in caller's context

                                       OK          Cancel
```

with the world. In this method, an object fetches its context object and stores it in a member variable. The sequence of activating a pooled object is shown in Figure 3-17.

Table 3-4 The *IObjectControl* Interface Methods

Method	Description
Activate	Allows an object to perform context-specific initialization whenever it is activated. This method is called by COM+ before any other methods are called on the object.
CanBePooled	Allows an object to let COM+ know whether it can be pooled for reuse.
Deactivate	Allows an object to perform whatever cleanup is necessary before being recycled or destroyed. This method is called by COM+ whenever an object is deactivated.

Figure 3-17 *Activating an object from the object pool.*

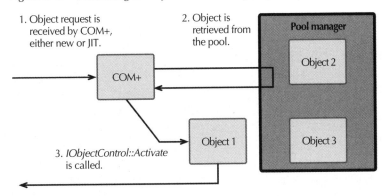

When the object is deactivated, COM+ calls the *IObjectControl:: Deactivate* method. This is the object's signal to release its resources. (Don't forget the context object if you fetched it in the *Activate* method.) After that, COM+ calls the *CanBePooled* method to see whether the object is capable of being placed back in the pool. If the object allows this, it goes into the pool; if not, it gets released. The deactivation sequence is shown in Figure 3-18.

When COM+ calls the *IObjectControl::Deactivate* method, it is the object's signal to release its resources.

Figure 3-18 *Deactivating an object and replacing it in the object pool.*

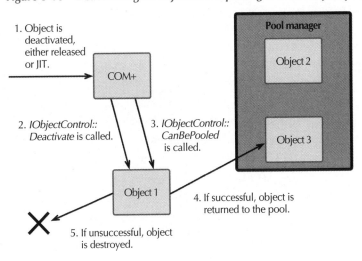

Object pooling nets you a performance profit only in cases where reinitializing an object is significantly faster than creating a brand-new one. This happens in two situations. First, if the object has no state at all to initialize, pulling the object out of a pool is usually significantly faster than dealing with a constructor. Second, pooling is faster when the object's state is expensive to initialize and when on deactivation you want to retain it instead of dump it. The latter case, as we've seen in the previous sections on JIT activation and state management, is exactly what you usually *don't* want.

Developing components for pooling requires meeting some fairly stringent requirements. A pooled object must implement the *IObjectControl* interface discussed earlier, in addition to whatever other interfaces it needs to carry out its work. In the *Activate* method, the object must ensure that it doesn't have any debris left over from previous operations that would hinder its operation as the new object that the client thinks it is. For example, the object would probably want to initialize the state of its member variables. In the *Deactivate* method, it must release any resources that it has allocated during its operation. In the *CanBePooled* method, it must examine the state of its soul and determine whether it can go back into the pool for reuse, or whether it has been so harshly used by the world that it needs to say farewell.

A pooled object must not care about which thread it receives its calls on—it must have no *thread affinity* or, shall we say, be "thread agnostic." A pooled object might be created from thread A when the COM+ run time initially fills the pool at startup time. It might be activated on thread B when it's taken from the pool and connected to a client. This means that the object must live in the multithreaded apartment (MTA) or neutral apartment (NA) (*ThreadingModel = Free, Both,* or *Neutral*). It can't live in a single-threaded apartment (STA) (*ThreadingModel = Apartment*). This rules out Visual Basic 6.0 and also the Microsoft Foundation Classes (MFC) as development environments for pooled components, as they contain thread affinity that you can't get rid of. This is why when using the Component Services snap-in, the Enable Object Pooling checkbox is grayed out for the *Bank.Account* component, which was written in Visual Basic. The snap-in sees the *ThreadingModel = Apartment* entry in the registry and says, "Aha, you can't support pooling, so I won't let the administrator turn it on." The box is enabled for the *Bank.Account.VC* component (see Figure 3-16) because that is marked with *Threading-Model = Both*. You can use the serialization mechanisms of COM+ to make it easier to develop the thread-agnostic component.

The pooled component must be aggregatable, as COM+ puts its own wrapper around the pooled component to keep track of it. This isn't hard; most tools do it for you transparently. The component must not aggregate any other pooled component, because the inner pooled component's wrapper would fight with the outer pooled component's wrapper. Again, this isn't terrible if you know at development time what's pooled and what isn't. In addition, the component must not aggregate the standard free-threaded marshaler, as this would break the threading mechanisms of COM+, which abstract away all those nasty threading details for you.

Compensating Transactions

Some operations are not reversible, so you really need to be sure you want to do them before you let them happen. Remember the two coworkers in the ThinkPad commercial on TV, frantically trying to "unsend, unsend" when their new ThinkPads got delivered just as they had sent their boss a nasty e-mail for not buying them?

Other operations can be undone by applying an equal but opposite operation. Suppose you buy a really cool 21-inch monitor with integrated stereo speakers. You pay for it on your Visa card and your account gets debited $1500. You get it home and surf like an Internet god until your spouse comes in and says, "It cost

A compensating transaction is an equal but opposite operation that undoes a previous operation.

HOW MUCH?" Under threat of beheading, you return the monitor the next day, thankful that you got to keep at least your cable modem. Visa does not tear up the first debit as though it had never happened. Instead, they apply an equal but opposite credit, and you see both debit and credit on your bill at the end of the month. The credit for the returned goods is called a *compensating transaction*.

Compensating transactions don't have the full isolation of classic transactions.

Compensating transactions have advantages and disadvantages. Their main disadvantage is that they lack the full isolation of a classic transaction. The credit limit in your Visa account went down when you bought the monitor and went back up again when you returned it. If the purchase pushed you over your credit limit, you couldn't buy other things on your Visa card until you returned the monitor and the compensating transaction had cleared. For reversible operations, however, the advantages of compensating transactions frequently outweigh this disadvantage. Compensating transactions often match well with real-life business processes, as in this example. They are often attractive when the alternative is a long or indeterminate resource lock time, such as when you are using queued components, which are described in Chapter 4.

Compensating Resource Managers

A Compensating Resource Manager (CRM) is useful and relatively easy to write.

As I hope you've seen by now, transactions are useful. Any type of resource manager that can't participate in transactions doesn't have a very promising career path. In the same way that you had to rewrite your proprietary utilities into COM components so you could access them easily from modern development tools, so you will also have to add transactional support if you want the proprietary utilities to be useful in COM+ enterprise applications. The problem is that RMs are hard to write, as shown by the intricate footwork they had to perform in the Sample Bank application or by the sample code provided in the MTS software development kit. It is reasonable to ask, "Hey, aren't many of the things RMs have to do common from one RM to another? And if that's so, isn't it possible to prefabricate large portions of the generic RM functionality that my RM can simply inherit?" That's what COM+ Compensating Resource Manager (CRM) support does.

You might think at first, as I did, that a CRM has something to do with compensating transactions. It doesn't, as you will see. This double use of the root word *compensate* is an unfortunate overloading of the nomenclature. A CRM is really any object that uses the specific CRM support provided by COM+. You can use this support to write a resource manager similar to the ones discussed in this chapter, or simply to inject your own code into different stages of the transaction commit process.

In order to write a CRM, you write two cooperating components, called the CRM Worker and the CRM Compensator. The CRM Worker does the actual management of the resources, such as posting debits to a charge account, by exposing whatever COM objects or other access modalities it requires for this purpose. The CRM Worker uses COM+'s CRM services to write records describing its operation (for example, "set balance of account 12345 to $500") to a durable log file. When the transaction closes, COM+ launches the CRM Compensator and passes it the outcome of the transaction along with the log file records written by the CRM Worker. The CRM Compensator reads the log file records and either does what it takes to make the operation permanent (in the case of a committed transaction) or does whatever it takes to undo it (in the case of an aborted transaction).

A CRM uses two components, a CRM Worker and a CRM Compensator.

The following example is based on the CRM sample application, which you can find on this book's Web site. This component's business logic is creating or deleting files in a transactional manner. A component called *CrmFilesWorker* provides the latter functionality via a method called *DeleteFile*, and marked as requiring a transaction. When a client creates an object of this class and calls this method, the worker moves the specified file to a temporary directory. If the transaction commits, CRM Compensator deletes the file from the temporary directory. If the transaction aborts, CRM Compensator moves it back to its original location.

The operation of the *CrmFilesWorker* object is shown in Figure 3-19. When the client calls the *DeleteFile* method (1), the CRM Worker first connects to the CRM Clerk (2), a utility object provided by COM+. It obtains the *ICrmLogControl* interface, whose methods are listed in Table 3-5.

Figure 3-19 *Operation of the* CrmFilesWorker *object.*

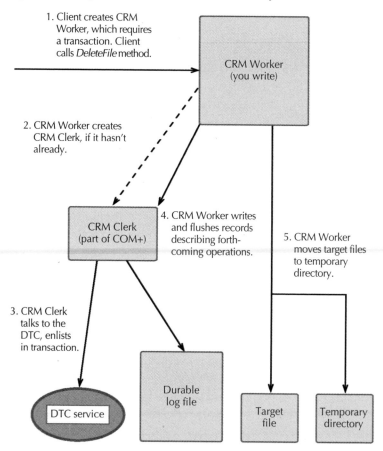

It then calls the clerk's *RegisterCompensator* method, telling the clerk which CRM Compensator to create when the DTC needs to close the transaction (not shown). The CRM Clerk then enlists in the transaction by calling the DTC as did SQL server in the Sample Bank application shown earlier (3). This operation need be performed only once for the life of the *CrmFilesWorker* object.

The CRM Worker uses the CRM Clerk's *WriteLogRecord* method to write records into a durable log file describing the work that it plans to do, and then uses the *ForceLog* method to make the log durable (4). The CRM Worker always writes the log file record before performing the actual operation. If it did things in the

The CRM Worker does its work and then uses the CRM Clerk to write durable log file records describing what it has done.

Table 3-5   The *ICrmLogControl* Interface Methods

Method	Description
RegisterCompensator	Tells CRM Clerk the Program ID of the CRM Compensator that knows how to commit or abort the work done by the CRM Worker when the transaction closes.
ForceLog	Immediately writes all records in the log to durable disk to ensure that they survive a crash.
ForgetLogRecord	Erases the last record written to the log file. This only works on the single last record written, and cannot be nested.
ForceTransactionToAbort	When called by the worker object, immediately forces the transaction to abort.
WriteLogRecord	Writes a record to the log using unstructured data. The log record does not become durable until *ForceLog* is called.
WriteLogRecordVariants	Write a record to the log by using VARIANT parameters. The log record does not become durable until *ForceLog* is called.
Get_TransactionUOW	Gets a unique ID identifying the transaction in progress.

opposite order (if it were to crash after moving but before logging the file) the system might be left in an inconsistent state. Next the CRM Worker performs the business logic of file deletion in a way that it knows the CRM Compensator is able to undo. In the sample, the CRM Worker moves the file to a different directory (5). If the worker ever encounters a problem it can't fix, it tells the clerk to abort the transaction by calling the *ForceTransactionToAbort* method (not shown).

When the transaction closes, the CRM Clerk participates in the DTC's two-phase commit protocol.

The operation of the *CrmFilesCompensator* object is shown in Figure 3-20. As we saw in Figure 3-19, the CRM Clerk is a system-provided resource manager that enlisted in the transaction. When the transaction closes, the clerk participates in the DTC's two-phase commit protocol discussed earlier. The CRM Clerk knows which compensator is required and creates it (1). The CRM Compensator is a COM object that supports the *ICrmCompensator* interface, whose methods are shown in Table 3-6. The clerk first calls *SetLogControl*, passing the CRM Compensator the *ICrmLogControl* interface that provides access to the log file (2). In the prepare phase of the transaction, the DTC notifies the CRM Clerk, which calls the CRM Compensator's *BeginPrepare, PrepareRecord,* and *EndPrepare* methods, passing the log file records

Figure 3-20 *The operation of the sample CRM Compensator.*

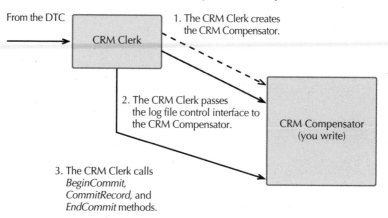

From the DTC

CRM Clerk

1. The CRM Clerk creates the CRM Compensator.

2. The CRM Clerk passes the log file control interface to the CRM Compensator.

CRM Compensator (you write)

3. The CRM Clerk calls *BeginCommit, CommitRecord,* and *EndCommit* methods.

written by the CRM Worker. If the CRM Compensator is unable to accomplish the necessary tasks of the prepare phase, it can abort the transaction at this stage by calling the *ICrmLogControl* interface's *ForceTransactionToAbort* method. The sample code doesn't do anything in the prepare phase of the transaction, so this is not shown on the diagram.

If the transaction commits, the DTC notifies the CRM Clerk, which then calls the CRM Compensator's *BeginCommit, CommitRecord,* and *EndCommit* methods (3). If the transaction aborts, the DTC calls *BeginAbort, AbortRecord,* and *EndAbort* (not shown).

Table 3-6   The *ICrmCompensator* Interface Methods

Method	Description
SetLogControl	Delivers the *ICrmLogControl* interface to the CRM Compensator, so it can write log file records
BeginPrepare	Notifies the CRM Compensator that DTC's prepare phase is commencing
EndPrepare	Notifies the CRM Compensator that DTC's prepare phase is ending; obtains the CRM Compensator's vote on committing the transaction
BeginCommit	Tells the CRM Compensator that DTC's commit phase is commencing
CommitRecord	Called once for each record in the log file written by this CRM Compensator or its associated CRM Worker during the transaction
EndCommit	Tells the CRM Compensator that DTC's commit phase is ending
BeginAbort	Tells the CRM Compensator that DTC's abort phase is beginning
AbortRecord	Called once for each record in the log file written by this CRM Compensator or its associated CRM Worker during the transaction
EndAbort	Tells the CRM Compensator that DTC's abort phase is ending

In both cases, the DTC passes the CRM Compensator the durable log file records written by the CRM Worker. The sample CRM Compensator ignores the begin and end methods. For each record in the log file, it either actually deletes the file if the transaction is committing, or restores it to its original place (undoing the delete) if the transaction is aborting.

Two somewhat tricky things should be kept in mind when you are writing a CRM component. The first is that the CRM Compensator can never know how many times it will be asked to perform the same operation. Suppose the CRM Compensator deletes the file when a transaction commits and then crashes before it can clear that record from the log file. The CRM Clerk will check its transaction log when it next starts up and feed the same records to the CRM Compensator again. The CRM Compensator needs to be written so that it produces the proper result if a log file record tells it to do something it's already done. That's easy in this case: the CRM Compensator simply ignores a request to delete a file that it can't find. But other operations, such as adding $100 to someone's bank account, don't work this way. If you do it three or four times because of repeated crash recovery, your customer will be very happy but your auditors won't. Instead, you probably want to write the log file record to set a customer's bank balance to a certain value, say, the value it originally had plus $100. An operation that produces the same result no matter how many times it runs is called *idempotent*, and that's how you need to structure your log file records.

The second design problem in writing a CRM component is knowing exactly when a transaction has committed. When a transaction successfully closes, the client application knows that all the operations will commit eventually, but it doesn't know *when* they have committed. Logically you might think that the RMs have completed all their operations when the two-phase commit process completes, but that isn't so. What happens if an RM crashes after successfully preparing but before receiving the commit notification from the DTC? It might not come back up for a week. It is up to the CRM to implement whatever software mechanisms it needs to provide your client with this knowledge, and up to the client to make use of it. The sample application does not demonstrate this technique.

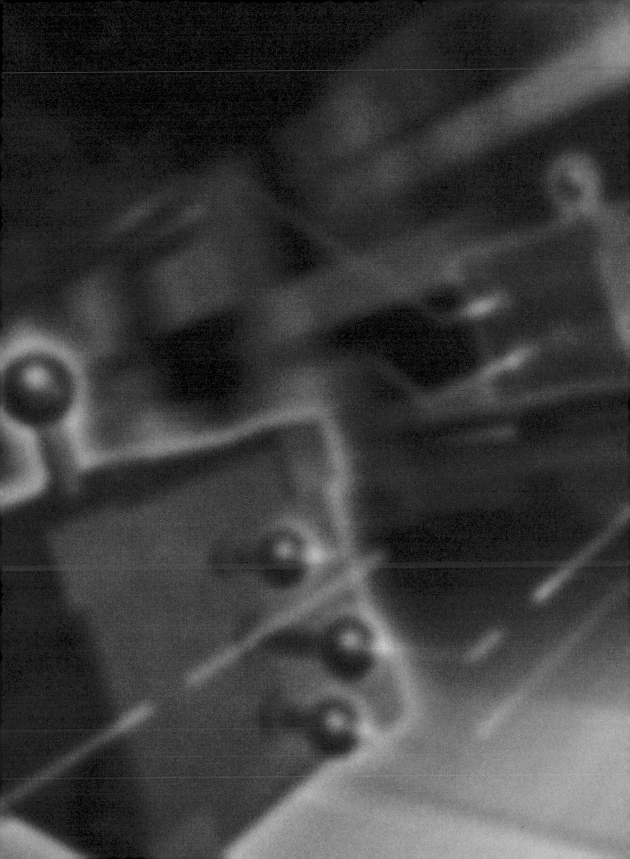

Chapter Four

Queued Components

Business Problem Background

When was the last time you telephoned someone and found him at his desk the first time you called? Been a while, hasn't it? When you fail to contact your party the first time, do you call every five minutes until he answers, getting nothing else done for the rest of the day? Of course not; no one can afford to do business that way. Instead, you leave a voice-mail message saying what you want: "Charlie, it's Dave, I'll meet you at the Plough and Stars Pub on Mass Ave. at five-thirty—bring the contract and your thirst. Call me at 555-1234 if you have a problem." Charlie picks up his voice mail at his convenience and either shows up or calls to cancel, probably leaving a message on your voice mail. That's enough for most business purposes, most of the time. Think about how many voice mails, e-mails, and snail mails you send, as opposed to how many face-to-face contacts or direct phone conversations you have. Asynchronous communications outstrip synchronous communications ten to one and are increasing every day.

> You do most of your day-to-day business communication with other humans in an asynchronous manner, via voice mail or e-mail.

The same problem arises in distributed computing. Suppose you are writing an application for customer service reps in a mail-order company. A rep takes an order from a customer over the phone and types it into her PC workstation. Some parts of this operation need to happen synchronously—for example, the product availability needs to be checked immediately, while the

> Synchronous communication in distributed applications often results in bottlenecks.

customer is still on the line. Other parts of the operation do not need to be completed synchronously—for example, there's no reason why the customer should wait on the phone while the rep sends the completed order to the shipping department's computer. What happens if the shipping department's computer is down for maintenance or is simply backlogged? The rep can't tell the customer to call back later—"Maybe the computer will be back up"—nor can the rep ignore other callers while she waits for the shipping computer to become available. Either option equals lost sales and lost customers.

We'd really like to have asynchronous communication between distributed applications, essentially computer-readable e-mail.

What we'd really like is some way for the rep's computer to leave a message for the shipping computer. We want voice mail or e-mail whose contents are readable by computer programs, so that when the shipping computer comes back up or digs out of its backlog, it will check its messages and handle them at that time. Communicating with the shipping department's computer does not *need* to happen synchronously, and since it doesn't need to, it *does* need *not to*. The rep's computer needs to know only that the message did in fact get placed in the outgoing mailbox from which it will eventually get delivered to the shipping computer.

Asynchronous communication means that we don't have to match the lifetimes of clients and servers to each other.

What advantages would such an architecture buy us? The most obvious is that we would no longer have to worry about server availability for operations that can be handled asynchronously. Neither client nor server would need to care about the lifetime of the other—only that enough server cycles are around to eventually handle all client requests (where *eventually* is defined as "soon enough for your business purposes") and that enough space exists in the inbox to hold all pending messages. This is important not just in the case where the server goes down temporarily from a malfunction: close to half of all PCs sold today are portable models. A user wants to take her PC somewhere, do some work with it, and later connect to a server to process the data generated during the offline operation. You already do this with e-mail messages that you create off line and then send when you find a convenient phone line. Extending this communication mechanism to programs doesn't require an enormous leap of imagination.

A disconnected architecture could also greatly improve performance and scalability of server applications by allowing more efficient use of server resources. For example, different server processes could be assigned different priorities. If the same server computer was used for both the in-stock products database and the shipping department, the administrator could assign a lower priority to the shipping process. That way, the server could offer fast response for the in-stock product queries that need to be handled while the customer waits and then catch up on the shipping requests in the middle of the night, when telephone customer demand fell off.

Another advantage is that the shipping request would contain all the information the server needed to process it. Suppose the server handled each new order by creating a new object at the beginning of the order process. The client application would call methods on this object, setting product number, quantity, shipping address, and so forth in response to the human end user's (in this case, the customer rep's) interaction with the user interface. The server would finally process and release the shipping object when the user clicked the Send button. The catch is that the server's shipping object would need to exist throughout the human operation, which means you have a lot of objects hanging around, using up memory and other resources, while waiting for humans to process information at human speeds. If the client application sent all its data in a single message, the object that processed that message would need to live only as long as it took the server to process the message. I find that requiring the students in my COM+ class at Harvard to submit their technical questions to me only through e-mail—and refusing to discuss code on the telephone—makes the students think carefully about what they are asking and assemble all the supporting data I need to help them before they send the request. It saves a lot of time for the server (me), thereby greatly increasing throughput.

Asynchronous communication also allows more efficient use of server resources.

All of this adds up to the same thing—it's a lot easier to write
most distributed applications if you do not need all the participants running at the same time. You could certainly write client
code that would check for the presence of a server and use it if
found, otherwise saving the data in the client's own database and
making the call when it detects a server again (put up a sticky
note to call Charlie when you get a chance, and then remember
to do it). However, developing this "store-and-forward" enterprise
infrastructure would take time and cost money. It would be much
better to inherit such an infrastructure from the operating system.
(Are you beginning to see a pattern in this book?)

Solution Architecture

Such an infrastructure is the Queued Components (hereafter QC,
formerly "real enough time") service of COM+. A client application creates a QC object using a special syntax to indicate that the
client wants the object to be queued. Once created, the client
application uses the object the same way it uses any other COM
object. The queued component exposes to its client a COM interface that looks more or less like any other COM interface.
Classic DCOM uses synchronous remote procedure call (RPC) to
squirt the bytes representing a COM call from one box to another,
as shown in Figure 4-1. However, with QC, the communication
between the client and the server is handled with Microsoft Message Queue Server (MSMQ) instead, as shown in Figure 4-2.

Figure 4-1   *Classic COM using RPC.*

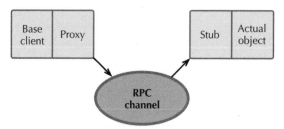

When a client creates a QC object, the client is connected not to the actual COM object, but rather to a call recorder. The client application makes COM calls as usual, but they get recorded on the client side instead of being squirted out immediately via RPC. When the object is deactivated, QC uses MSMQ to asynchronously send the bundle of recorded COM calls to the server on which the actual object lives. When the server feels like it, it uses MSMQ to read in a bundle of COM calls sent by a client. The server activates a player object that creates the actual COM object and plays the recorded calls into it.

You don't have to think about the details of MSMQ—they've been abstracted away. Your client application simply makes COM calls the way it's used to doing, and the underlying system infrastructure makes the right thing happen, even though the client and server aren't necessarily running at the same time.

Writing queued components is just as easy. You merely write a COM component as usual, with whatever tools you like (Microsoft Visual Basic, Microsoft Visual J++, Active Template Library [ATL], and so forth). You have to live with a few restrictions on the semantics of your interfaces, since you can't rely on output parameters (described in more detail later in the "Interface Design" section of this chapter), but these changes are relatively minor. You then install your component in a COM+ application, using the Component Services snap-in to mark its interfaces as queued. COM+ will then take care of listening for incoming

> Queued Components is a run-time service of COM+ that provides asynchronous communication by using MSMQ as the underlying transport mechanism for COM calls.

> You write a COM component for queuing in much the same way as a nonqueued component.

Figure 4-2 *COM with a QC object using MSMQ.*

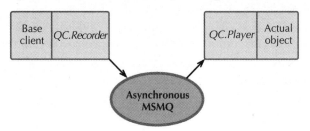

MSMQ messages from clients and calling your component's methods when they arrive. Again, the nasty details of becoming asynchronous have been abstracted away by the QC service. The component you write incorporates your business logic and takes advantage of the queuing infrastructure supplied by the operating system.

MSMQ is Microsoft's run-time service for asynchronous messaging.

MSMQ is a rich set of run-time services that allows applications on different machines to send and receive asynchronous messages to and from each other. It first appeared in the Microsoft Windows NT 4.0 Option Pack in December 1997 and is an integral part of Windows 2000. An application that wants to receive messages creates a queue, a persistent administrative structure known to the operating system and conceptually similar to a mailbox. An application that wants to send a message to another application locates this queue, either through system services or through application-based foreknowledge, and uses the MSMQ service to send a message to it. An MSMQ message can contain plain text or COM objects that support the *IPersistStream* interface. Messages pass through the network topology configured by the system administrator until they reach the recipient machine. If the recipient machine is not running when the message is sent, the message is buffered by the sending machine's operating system until the recipient machine starts running. An application can receive MSMQ messages by either polling its queue or using callback notification.

MSMQ contains a rich set of features to support this basic message delivery service. For example, the sender of a message can specify that the message expire and be deleted if it does not reach the recipient's queue within a certain time interval or if it is not read from the queue by the receiving application within a different time interval. The sender can ask to be notified when the message is received, only if it expires unread, or not at all. For a more detailed description of MSMQ, see David Chappell's forthcoming book from Microsoft Press, *Understanding Microsoft Windows 2000*

Distributed Services, or his article "Microsoft Message Queue Is a Fast, Efficient Choice for Your Distributed Application" (*Microsoft Systems Journal,* July 1998).

Since MSMQ is a good foundation, why do we want the higher level of abstraction provided by QC? Three reasons come to mind: First, the higher level of abstraction presented by QC is easier to program than raw MSMQ, in the same way that Visual Basic is easier to program than Visual C++. The higher level of abstraction takes care of the nasty details that are the same in most implementations anyway. Second, you don't have to learn a new programming model. You probably already use COM in many places in your application—for example, when you use ADO to connect to databases. With QC, you don't have to change mindsets to program MSMQ. Third, the COM components that you write can be used either asynchronously through the QC service or, if you prefer, synchronously through DCOM. You have the flexibility of using queued access to a component where it makes sense and non-queued access to the same binary component where you need it.

The main drawback of using QC instead of raw MSMQ is the same that you find with any higher level of abstraction: a loss of fine-grained control. You can't do absolutely everything through QC that you could if you were using MSMQ directly, in the same way that you can't get quite everything done in Visual Basic that you can in Visual C++. You can handle most cases most of the time, and that's usually enough to make lots of money. Since the greatest constraint on any software development project is time-to-market, you don't really have any economic choice but to use any higher level of abstraction that shortens the development time. Ask yourself how much programming you've done lately in assembly language. Programming raw MSMQ doesn't take that long. Programming QC is an order of magnitude faster.

Using Queued Components makes MSMQ easier to use.

Simplest QC Example

A QC workflow example begins here.

Let's look at the QC way of writing a mail-order shipping application similar to the one discussed in the opening sections of this chapter. The following discussion is based on the QC Shipping sample application available on this book's Web page. The key point to keep in mind as you follow the example is that, as with so many parts of COM+, neither the client developer nor the component developer needs to do very much to tie into the infrastructure (in this case, queued messaging) inherited from the operating system. In the example discussed below, all the component author has to do is use the Component Services snap-in to mark the component's interfaces as being queued. All the client developer has to do is create the component in a particular way that causes COM+ to treat it as queued. The rest of the complex dance is performed by the operating system. Write your business logic in the form of a COM component, and then let go and let COM+.

A diagram of the sample application is shown in Figure 4-3.

Figure 4-3 *Architecture of the QC Shipping sample application.*

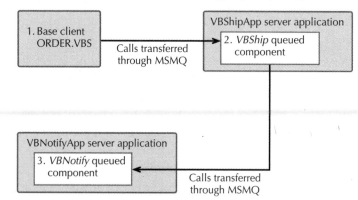

QC uses standard COM components.

The base client for this demo is a VBScript interpreter, running a script called ORDER.VBS (1). It simulates the order entry process by creating a QC object called *VBShip* and calling its COM methods to simulate the entry of an order (2). Since *VBShip* is a queued component, MSMQ transmits the COM calls made by the base client. In a commercial installation, *VBShip* would probably reside on a different machine. The *VBShip* component uses another queued component, *VBNotify*, to report the status of the shipment order to a hypothetical administrative application (3).

The administrator first sets up the required applications and components by using the Component Services snap-in. The administrator creates a new COM+ server application, here called VBShipApp, and marks it as queued, as shown in Figure 4-4.

The administrator uses the Component Services snap-in to set up the required applications and components.

Figure 4-4 *Marking an application as queued.*

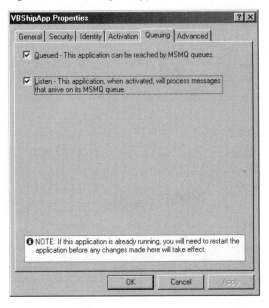

This causes COM+ to create message queues for the use of any queued components that are added to the application. You can use the MSMQ snap-in to view these queues, as shown in Figure 4-5.

Figure 4-5 *The MSMQ snap-in showing queues created by a COM+ queued application.*

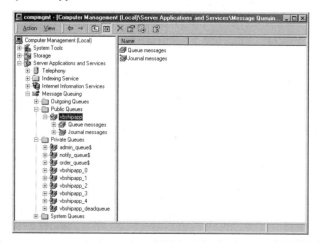

Checking the Listen box tells COM+ that when the application is launched, COM+ should activate the listener service that it needs to receive incoming calls through MSMQ.

You use the Component Services snap-in to mark your application and interfaces as supporting queuing services.

The administrator next adds components to the application. The interfaces of the components also need to be marked as queued, as shown in Figure 4-6.

Figure 4-6 *Marking an interface as queued.*

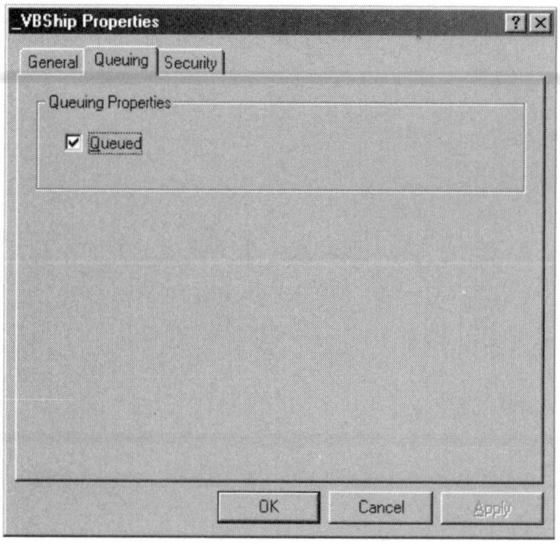

This tells COM+ that it should expect to receive incoming calls to this interface through MSMQ. This setting only affects the incoming calls received by the interface. It does not affect the outgoing calls made by that component to other components, which can be any mix of queued and nonqueued. The checkbox will not be enabled unless the interface has been designed in such a manner as to allow it to be accessed in a queued fashion, essentially removing any kind of output parameters, as described later in this chapter.

The VBScript used by the base client is shown in Figure 4-7, and the flow of operations triggered by its use is shown in Figure 4-8.

The base client does not create the *VBShip* object via the *CreateObject* or *CoCreateInstance* functions; these instruments are too blunt. Instead, it uses the Visual Basic function *GetObject*, whose C++ equivalent is *CoGetObject* (1). This function uses a text string

A QC client uses a queue moniker to create an object that it wants to access through MSMQ.

Figure 4-7 *The VBScript listing for the base client in the QC Shipping sample application.*

```
Dim Ship
Set Ship =
    GetObject("queue:/new:VBShipProj.VBShip")

Ship.CustomerID = 1111
Ship.OrderID    = 2222
Ship.LineItem 12, "Drummers drumming"
Ship.LineItem 11, "Pipers piping"
Ship.LineItem 10, "Lords a leaping"
Ship.LineItem  9, "Ladies dancing"
Ship.LineItem  8, "Maids a milking"
Ship.LineItem  7, "Swans a swimming"
Ship.LineItem  6, "Geese a laying"
Ship.LineItem  5, "Gold rings"
Ship.LineItem  4, "Calling birds"
Ship.LineItem  3, "French hens"
Ship.LineItem  2, "Turtledoves"
Ship.LineItem  1, "A partridge in a pear tree"

Ship Process
```

A moniker is a COM object that knows how to locate another COM object based on a text string passed to the moniker.

to activate a series of *monikers* to create the *VBShip* object. A moniker is a COM object that knows how to locate another COM object based on a text string passed to the moniker. Monikers have been around since the early days of OLE, where they were originally used for compound document linking. The use of monikers in QC is discussed in more detail later in the "Using the Queue Moniker" section of this chapter.

Figure 4-8   *The* **VBShip** *object connected to* **QC.Recorder.**

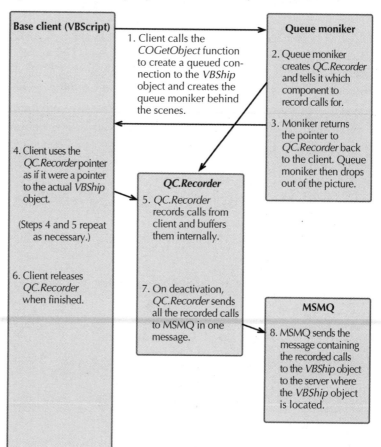

By using the moniker instead of calling *CreateObject*, the client doesn't actually create a *VBShip* object (2). Instead, the client is connected to *QC.Recorder*, a COM+ utility component that is part of the run-time system (3). (You can see it in the COM+ Utilities application in the Component Services snap-in, as shown in Figure 4-9.) While this technique may sound exotic, it's really nothing new. You know that when a client creates an object, it often receives a proxy instead of a direct connection to the object. Even creating a proxy at run time, based on type library information, is not new; dual interfaces do this all the time. You can simply think of the recorder as a different kind of proxy, one that squirts its calls into MSMQ instead of RPC.

A QC client receives a connection to *QC.Recorder*.

Figure 4-9 *The Component Services snap-in showing* QC.Recorder *and* QC.ListenerHelper *in the COM+ Utilities application.*

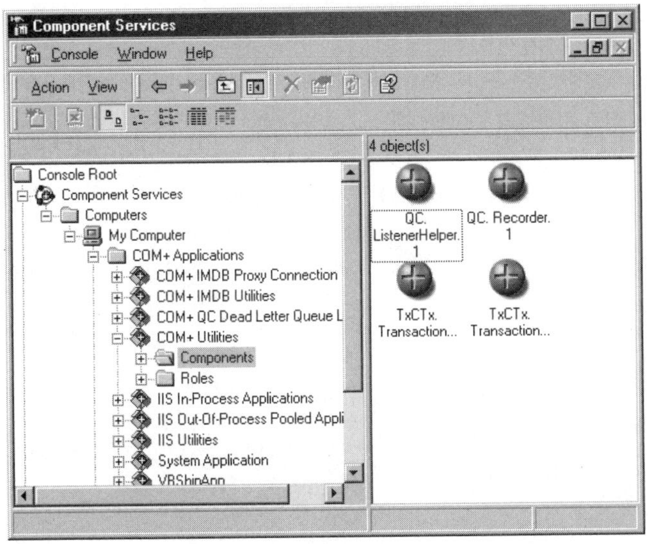

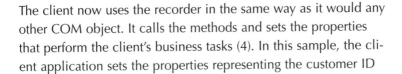

The client now uses the recorder in the same way as it would any other COM object. It calls the methods and sets the properties that perform the client's business tasks (4). In this sample, the client application sets the properties representing the customer ID and the order ID, orders a number of seasonal items, and then calls the method *Process* to tell the component to process the order as entered.

The recorder knows, from reading the type library describing the *VBShip* component, what methods and properties *VBShip* contains and what their parameters are. When the client makes its calls, the recorder catches them and stores them internally (5) until the entire series of COM calls is complete and the object is deactivated. In the example, this occurs when the object goes out of scope at the end of the script (6). When this happens, the recorder transmits all of its recorded calls in one MSMQ message (7). MSMQ then transmits the message containing these recorded calls to the machine on which the *VBShip* object is actually located (8).

When the client makes calls on its queued object, the calls are recorded for later transmission by MSMQ.

There is no way to flush the recorder's call buffer without deactivating the object. However, by using a queued component, the client is saying that it doesn't care exactly when the calls get processed. So this really shouldn't be a problem. Just remember when you are writing a client application that your QC calls won't even start their journey to the server until the object is deactivated. The message containing the client's recorded calls has now been handed over to MSMQ, which will transmit the calls to the recipient machine.

MSMQ automatically forwards the recording of the COM calls to the server machine.

The transmission happens in accordance with the administrative configuration of MSMQ and the network topology of the installation on which the client and server are running. If both are on the same network and running and not too busy, the message can take a ballpark figure of perhaps 10 milliseconds to arrive at the recipient queue. If the two machines are disconnected, MSMQ will automatically store the message containing the recorded COM calls and automatically forward them the next time the machines are connected. MSMQ uses a secure protocol in the forwarding process, making sure that messages are acknowledged by the recipient before being erased from the sender's queue so that messages don't get lost. Don't forget, however, that you need to worry about the client machine physically disappearing or breaking down before the recorded calls get forwarded.

The process of receiving calls is shown in Figure 4-10. QC provides another utility component, called *QC.ListenerHelper* (shown previously in the Component Services snap-in in Figure 4-9). This listener must be activated to receive incoming QC calls (1). The listener can be activated either by the system administrator using the Component Services snap-in, as shown in Figure 4-4, or by a utility program using the COM+ catalog administrative objects as described in Chapter 2. The *QC.ListenerHelper* component

Recorded COM calls are caught by a system-provided listener and passed to the actual object by a system-provided player.

Figure 4-10 *Reception and playback of QC calls.*

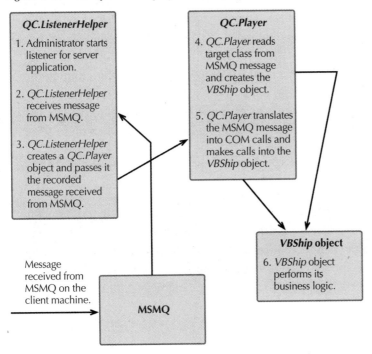

connects to MSMQ and listens for incoming messages using MSMQ's callback architecture (2). Any messages present in the queue at startup will be processed first. When the listener receives a message from MSMQ, it creates an object of the *QC.Player* class (3). This object dequeues the data received from MSMQ, creates the actual *VBShip* object on the server side (4), and makes the actual calls into it (5). And last but not least, the *VBShip* object does its work (6). Think of this player as a COM stub for the *VBShip* object.

Design of Queued Components

Designing queued components to operate successfully within the constraints imposed by COM+ requires advance thought and planning.

That the logistics of using QC are fairly easy and seem to require little thought is a misleading view. Again, the religious analogy from Chapter 2 holds true. The direct interaction of our queued components with COM+ is indeed simple and doesn't take much effort, similar to attending synagogue on Saturday or mosque on Friday. However, living day-to-day life in accordance with the constraints imposed by those religious beliefs (such as making sure that kosher or halal food is available to your children three times a day, seven days a week) requires advance thought and planning. So does designing queued components to operate successfully within the constraints imposed by COM+ require advance thought and planning.

Interface Design

All the COM code you've ever written in your life has probably been written with the underlying assumption, frequently unstated, that a client was always talking synchronously to the object, perhaps through the unseen mediation of a proxy and stub. But the other guy was there and was listening when you spoke and would return information to you using output parameters passed in your COM calls. Each COM call had at least the potential for bidirectional communication, through a returned *HRESULT* if nothing else. The lifetimes of client and object had to overlap.

That's no longer the case in QC. All interfaces used in QC need to be unidirectional, so they can be recorded and played back at a later time. This means that you can't use any output or input/output parameters in the interfaces of your QC components, because you don't know when the server will get to your request or whether you'll even be running at that point. The .IDL flags *[out]*, *[in, out]*, and *[retval]* are taboo. For example, the following method, standard in synchronous COM, will not work in QC because the last parameter is used for output:

```
SendOrderAndGetConfirmation([in] ProductID,
    [in] Quantity,
                    [out, retval] Confirmation)
```

In QC, this method must be rewritten to use input parameters only:

```
SendOrder([in] ProductID, [in] Quantity)
```

The COM+ catalog checks a component's type library when the component is installed in an application. If the component meets these criteria, according to the description in the type library, it is deemed to be queueable and the queuing properties user interface is enabled. Otherwise, the user interface will be grayed out.

Not only must the parameters of a queued component be unidirectional, they must be passed by value. Persistent COM objects, those that support the *IPersistStream* interface, can also be passed. This is discussed in more detail in the following section.

> The methods exposed by QC components must use input parameters only.

> Parameters passed to a QC method must be passed by value.

Writing components in Visual Basic can present a problem here. By default, Visual Basic passes all parameters by reference, using the [in, out] attribute, which QC does not allow. If you want to use Visual Basic to write queued components, you must specify the *ByVal* attribute for passing parameters.

Data passed in calls to queued components must be self-sufficient.

A more subtle limitation of QC is that the series of COM calls transmitted by a client during a session with a component needs to be self-sufficient. Think about the voice-mail example in the first part of this chapter. I left my phone number and the address of the pub even though Charlie probably knew them. Since the communication was asynchronous, he couldn't ask me for them if he didn't. You need to do the same thing with the design of your interfaces: make certain that the client is forced to directly pass everything the server needs to know, because the server can't make callbacks to the client later to request missing pieces of information. For example, it is common practice for a COM client to pass data sets to an object in the form of collections or enumerator objects. The client then becomes in essence the server of the collection or enumerator object, and the original object becomes its client. The server makes a call to the client to fetch each item in the collection. This will not work in QC because the lifetimes of the two sides can't be required to overlap. If a client has a set of data values that it needs to pass to the server object, it could use multiple recorded COM calls, as shown in the VBScript example earlier in this chapter. Alternatively, you could pass the data as a dimensioned array.

QC methods must not return application-specific error codes.

Finally, QC methods must not return application-specific error result codes to their callers. Remember how calls are recorded on the client and then played back on the server some indeterminate amount of time later? The code that implements the component's business logic and that would generate that error result code isn't available at the time the client makes the call and receives the result code. The return value that the client receives indicates only that the call has or has not been successfully recorded.

Receiving Output

Obviously we can do only so much with one-way communication. Nobody sells many write-only memory chips. We need to discuss the different mechanisms for receiving output from a QC server. Several choices are available, depending on your business process requirements. Consider the three classes of user—the optimist, the pessimist, and the pragmatist.

There are three philosophies about receiving output in QC.

An optimist never requires any output as the result of a QC call, other than the return code from the client-side *QC.Recorder* saying that the call has been successfully recorded. The client's job is finished when the message is recorded, in the same way that writing a thank-you note to your mother is finished when you put it in the mailbox. You don't usually spend much time finding out whether she got it. This worldview works well for applications whose only task is input; for example, a grocery store application in which a stock clerk carries a handheld PC on her regular rounds to record the number of bags of potato chips on the shelves. The handheld PC performs input recording only. Once the figures are transmitted, the handheld PC doesn't care about them anymore— as long as they do eventually get delivered, of course, and that's the operating system's problem. The clerk does not require a confirmation number for each input bag of potato chips. Any later checks that you want to put in the system are carried out by other applications using other channels.

An optimist never cares about output.

A pessimist requires a response for every call, similar to RPC. Don't do this. If you find yourself operating in this mode, you're missing the whole point of QC and need to change your mindset. If something needs to be synchronous, make it synchronous. *Vive la difference!*

A pessimist wants output after every call.

A pragmatist requires response messages for some calls but not for others. You would use this approach when the client has a continuing interest in the successful completion of the downstream business process triggered by the QC call. Consider what

A pragmatist wants confirmation of downstream business processes.

happens when you order something by phone. The order taker types in your order and gives you an order confirmation number. If your order doesn't arrive by the time it's supposed to, you call customer service and give them the confirmation number so they can track it. That's the sort of thing that a pragmatic QC client would like to receive from a QC server.

The client has two ways of telling the server how to respond.

Since the order entry is asynchronous, the order response should also be asynchronous, using a QC response object to communicate with the client machine. The server could certainly be hardwired to always respond to a specific object on a specific machine, as is the QC Shipping sample application provided on this book's Web site, but this solution isn't very flexible. The client has two ways of telling the server how to respond when it gets around to it. First, the client can provide a string containing its machine name as a parameter to the original QC interface. This strategy is diagrammed in Figure 4-11.

Figure 4-11 *Passing a string containing callback information.*

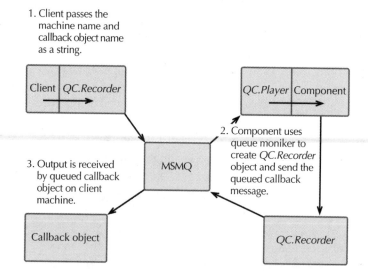

1. Client passes the machine name and callback object name as a string.

Client | QC.Recorder

QC.Player | Component

2. Component uses queue moniker to create *QC.Recorder* object and send the queued callback message.

3. Output is received by queued callback object on client machine.

MSMQ

Callback object

QC.Recorder

The server will use the string in its own queue moniker when creating the callback object. Passing data to the moniker in this fashion is described later, in the section "Using the Queue Moniker."

A QC application can receive output by passing location strings to its server.

The second strategy is shown in Figure 4-12. Instead of a string, the client application passes an actual QC object on its own machine for the server to use as a callback. Although, in general, nonpersistent COM objects can't be passed as parameters in QC, passing another queued object for use as a callback is supported as a special case. The client application uses a queue moniker to create a QC object of the callback class on its local machine and gets a recorder that mimics the callback object (1). It passes this recorder as a parameter to an outgoing QC call, essentially passing the first recorder to a second recorder that is handling the outgoing call (2). The outgoing QC call marshals the callback QC object into its outgoing call buffer, after which the client can release the callback object. When *QC.Player* on the server plays its

A QC application can receive output by passing callback queued components as parameters to its server.

Figure 4-12 *Passing a queued object containing callback information.*

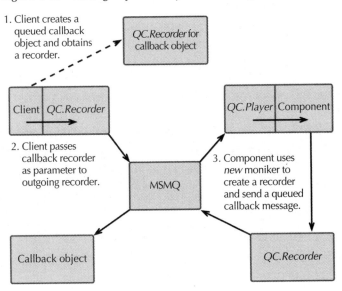

incoming calls, it will unmarshal the reference to the client-side callback object and create a new recorder on the server side that is pointed at the right queue on the client side (3). It's much easier to see how this works in the diagram.

When considering mechanisms for output, give some thought to avoiding the necessity for output altogether.

Finally, when considering mechanisms for output, give some thought to avoiding the necessity for output altogether. For example, the telephone order taker might want to generate order numbers on the client PC rather than wait for the numbers to come back from the server, perhaps using a globally unique identifier (GUID) to ensure that they are unique. As I said before, even though it might seem familiar, QC is a new mindset, and adjusting to it will take some thought.

Use of Transactions with Queued Components

In Chapter 3, we saw how useful transactions can be in solving the problems of maintaining data integrity in distributed systems. Many of these same problems also apply to asynchronous operations. Accordingly, queued components are capable of using transactions, both externally, to cooperate with other components, and internally, for reliability.

MSMQ, which underlies QC, is a resource manager, which means that it can enlist in transactions. For example, with MSMQ, within the context of a transaction components can make changes to tables in SQL Server and queue messages. If the transaction commits, the SQL changes will become permanent and the MSMQ messages will be sent. If the transaction aborts, the SQL changes and the MSMQ messages will be discarded. This sequence is illustrated in Figure 4-13.

MSMQ can participate in transactions as a COM+ resource manager.

For more information on the transactional abilities of the underlying MSMQ system, see "Use MSMQ and MTS to Simplify the Building of Transactional Applications" by Mark Bukovec and Dick Dievendorff in the July 1998 issue of *Microsoft Systems Journal*.

Figure 4-13 *MSMQ participating in a transaction.*

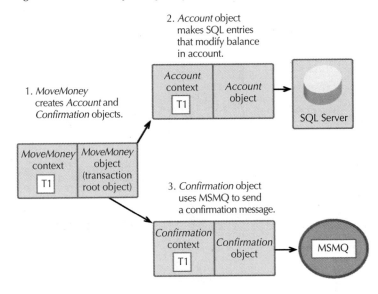

The transaction support of the underlying MSMQ transport mechanism is available to QC. The *QC.Recorder* utility component takes on the same transaction attribute as its client. If a client creates a queued component and receives the recorder within the context of an existing transaction, the transaction is propagated to the recorder. When the recorder is deactivated and sends its bundle of calls to MSMQ, it does so within the context of this transaction, so MSMQ buffers the message pending the outcome of the transaction. If the transaction commits, MSMQ transmits the message containing the recorded calls to its recipient. If the transaction aborts, perhaps because a different component was unhappy about something else, MSMQ throws the message away and the recorded COM calls never happened. A diagram of this is shown in Figure 4-14.

QC uses transactions on the server side as well. The dequeuing operation is transacted for reliability. Suppose *QC.Player* dequeued a message, and then some idiot knocked the computer's plug out of the wall. If the message queue were not protected by a

> The transactional support of the underlying MSMQ is available to QC.

Figure 4-14 A QC object participating in a transaction.

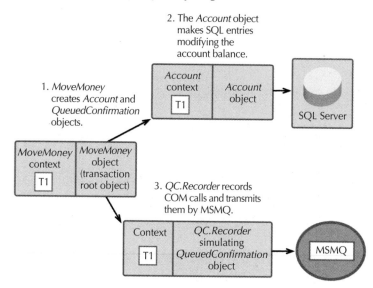

2. The *Account* object makes SQL entries modifying the account balance.

1. *MoveMoney* creates *Account* and *QueuedConfirmation* objects.

Account context
T1
Account object

SQL Server

MoveMoney context
T1
MoveMoney object (transaction root object)

3. *QC.Recorder* records COM calls and transmits them by MSMQ.

Context
T1
QC.Recorder simulating *QueuedConfirmation* object

MSMQ

transaction, the message would be lost. However, since the dequeuing operation is transacted, the transaction will abort when the machine's power comes back on, and the message will be put back in the queue. If the downstream components are also transacted, we are assured that the message representing the incoming COM calls is processed exactly once. This process is shown in Figure 4-15.

In QC, what happens if an operation fails on the server side?

Transacted playback has other advantages as well. In QC, what happens if an operation fails on the server side? Although the client isn't around to retry the operation, the automatic use of transactions by QC can do it. Suppose the Sample Bank application in Chapter 3 was triggered not by a synchronous user interface but by an asynchronous bundle of incoming QC calls. The server would dequeue the incoming message and create the *MoveMoney* object. Unlike the Chapter 3 example, however, *MoveMoney* would not be the root of the transaction. Instead, the transacted component *QC.ListenerHelper* is the root. Since *MoveMoney* also requires a transaction, *QC.ListenerHelper*'s transaction is propagated to the *MoveMoney* object when the latter is created. If the *MoveMoney* operation aborts for some reason, the message that triggered it is requeued. Maybe the machine that the *MoveMoney* object or one of its accounts needed to do its work will be back up the next time the *MoveMoney* object is triggered. If the operation had not been transacted, you would have had to write your own retry mechanism. Now you can inherit one from the operating system.

Some incoming messages can cause a transaction to abort repeatedly; for example, a message from an older remote client that doesn't have the current database schema. The shipping component tries to enter the bad record into its database, the database

If the *MoveMoney* operation aborts for some reason, the message that triggered it is requeued.

Figure 4-15 *A QC object participating in a transaction.*

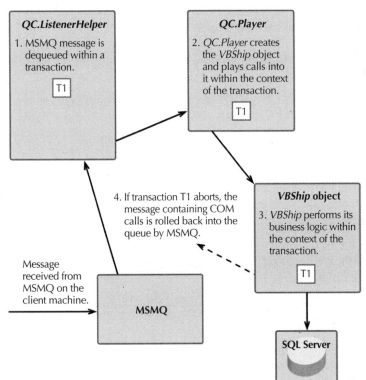

complains, the component aborts, the message goes back on the queue. Next time the component dequeues the same message, the same thing happens, ad infinitum. You can't allow your entire enterprise application to hang because of one "poison" message. Fortunately, the automatic retry mechanism contains a built-in solution.

When an incoming message aborts, QC moves the message to a different queue so that it doesn't block the others. The QC infrastructure currently creates six private queues for this purpose, as shown previously in Figure 4-5. QC then periodically retries the message. An aborted message starts in queue 0 and moves upward as future retries continue to fail. Higher numbers indicate longer intervals between retries. The number of retries at each level and the time intervals between them have not been finalized at the time of this writing. They will probably not be configurable, at least in the first release of COM+.

QC uses transactions to make sure that all the calls succeed together or fail together.

After using up all its retries at lower levels, QC moves the incoming message to the dead queue, from which it will not be tried again. It is up to you to write whatever administrative code you need to check this queue and deal with its problems in whatever manner is appropriate to your business operation. You might call a human operator to fix the problem, say, by turning on the server machine that the downstream operation is trying to reach and moving the messages back to a lower queue. An administrative tool called the MessageMover is available for help with this operation. For the hypothetical obsolete client that I proposed, you might gather diagnostic info and delete the message. Obviously, dealing with an aborted order for a hot cup of coffee will require different procedures than would dealing with an aborted order for a nuclear launch. COM+ did its best for you; now you're on your own.

The robustness and versatility of using transactions for QC messages comes at the price of slower performance—although, since all the recording is done in-process, the client will still finish its task more quickly than if it were actually talking to a remote server via DCOM. In a distributed system, reliability is the preferable quality, especially since, by using QC, you've said in effect that a response time of "eventually" is acceptable. However, sometimes microseconds make a difference. In this case, it is possible, but somewhat difficult and awkward, to turn off the transactioning mechanism used by QC.

Queues in MSMQ are either transacted or nontransacted. This attribute is set at the time of the queue's creation and cannot be changed later. The queues created by the Component Services snap-in when you mark the application as queued are always transacted. You must use the MSMQ snap-in to create a new nontransacted queue with the name of a COM+ application that hasn't yet been marked as queued. If you then use the Component Services snap-in to mark that application as queued, it will use the nontransacted one you just created, rather than creating a new transacted one. All of QC's internal operations will then use the nontransacted queues and consequently execute much faster. If you don't care about coordinating your operations with those of other components, and if a power failure wouldn't kill you, and if you don't mind the extra administrative effort, you might be able save a few extra microseconds by turning off transactioning. I don't think it will usually be worth the trouble. But if you try it, make sure that all of your components in your application are nontransacted. Mixing nontransacted queues with transacted queues raises interesting correctness issues.

It is possible to turn off transactions in QC, but think twice before you do it.

Security of Queued Components

A queued component has the same security requirements as a nonqueued component. When a server receives a queued request saying that Dr. Jones wants to prescribe morphine for patient Smith, it still has to answer the same two questions: Is it really Dr. Jones making the request, and is Dr. Jones allowed to prescribe morphine? We also have the same requirement of making sure that no unauthorized person even sees the request for morphine—maybe someone would steal the unconscious patient's drugs.

The security mechanism in a disconnected, asynchronous system works on different principles from that in a connected, synchronous system. The COM+ role-based security described in Chapter 2 abstracts away these differences. If you stick to it, you will find that the same security code will work for both the queued and non-queued components. You're going to find that working at a lower level of the security infrastructure is tricky in QC. For example, Kerberos security tickets expire after a certain amount of time, and caring about time is anathema to the QC world. At the very least, you will wind up writing different code for synchronous and asynchronous security, an effort you don't really want to make.

The first question is authentication—is the caller really who he says he is? The challenge-response mechanism used for DCOM doesn't work with MSMQ, because the former requires the components to communicate synchronously, which the latter cannot guarantee. MSMQ uses a different authentication, based on digital signatures that travel with a message. When MSMQ sends a message, it attaches a digital signature to the message. It also calculates and encrypts a hash value of the message's contents to prevent tampering. When the message arrives at the receiving end, MSMQ checks the signature, recalculates the hash value, and places the message in the dead queue if either is not correct.

When the client creates a QC object, QC turns on MSMQ's authentication mechanism if the server application on the client machine has any security settings enabled or if the client specifically requests authentication by specifying the *AuthLevel* attribute in its call to *GetObject*. This causes MSMQ to send the message containing the bundle of COM calls with a digital signature and an encrypted hash value. If its role-based security feature is enabled, the server application requires the client to send its message with MSMQ's authentication. Any incoming messages that do not carry the signature saying that MSMQ is sure of the sender's identity, or whose hash values indicate that they were tampered with in transit, are placed in the dead queue.

The second question is that of authorization—now that we are sure who the caller is, is the caller allowed to do what he's asking to do? COM+ abstracts this problem away quite nicely with the role-based security checking described in Chapter 2, and QC fully supports this mechanism. Each QC call contains security information about the caller, specifying the roles to which the caller belongs (and thus the actions the caller is allowed to take). Any administrative or programmatic role-checks that the server components contained will work properly without modification whether the caller is synchronous or queued.

What about the transmission of sensitive data—essentially all data—on the wire? Unless you can secure every inch of network wire, and in reality nobody can, every piece of data you send could wind up on the front page of *The National Enquirer* tomorrow. Most applications will want some form of encryption for at least some operations. Synchronous DCOM provided this capability when you set the authentication level to Packet Privacy. MSMQ provides a privacy-level setting. The client must set the *PrivLevel* attribute to the value *MQMSG_PRIV_LEVEL_BODY* in the call to *GetObject* that creates the recorder. Setting this privacy level causes MSMQ to encrypt the message containing the bundled calls recorded for an object before transmitting the message. The *EncryptAlgorithm* attribute allows you to specify the algorithm used for this encryption.

Using the Queue Moniker

MSMQ is a feature-rich service. An important part of designing the QC system was determining which features of the underlying MSMQ would be exposed at the QC abstraction level and how that exposure should be accomplished. The mechanism shown here is the result of much skull sweat.

An important part of designing the QC system was determining which features of the underlying MSMQ would be exposed at the QC abstraction level.

A client creates a queued connection to a component by calling the function *CoGetObject* or its Visual Basic equivalent *GetObject*. An example of the latter was discussed previously and shown in Figure 4-7. The line that activated *QC.Recorder* to record calls and transmit them to the server was

```
GetObject("queue:/new:VBShipProj.VBShip")
```

The function *GetObject* uses monikers to create the recorder that simulates the presence of the actual component. Using this mechanism instead of the classic *CoCreateInstance* or *Create-Object* functions solves two problems. First, it lets us specify the initial state of the object—for example, the computer name to which the recorder will deliver its messages—at the time we create it. Second, it allows us to use the same binary component in both queued and nonqueued situations.

Think of a moniker as a class factory to which a function can pass an initialization string so that the moniker can return a new object with its initial settings already made.

A moniker is a type of object that knows how to locate or create other objects. A *class factory* is another type of object that knows how to create other objects, but no method exists for passing a class factory any information about the object's initial settings. If you think of a moniker as a class factory to which a function can pass an initialization string so that the moniker can return a new object with its initial settings already made, you will have the right idea. The process by which a moniker creates an object is known as *binding*.

Different types of monikers exist, each of which creates an object based on different types of input data. When the base client calls *GetObject*, the function looks at the supplied text string and attempts to find a moniker of the type named by the leftmost substring before the colon, in this case, "queue". This name is a *ProgID* in the registry, as shown in Figure 4-16.

Figure 4-16 *A queue moniker entry in the registry.*

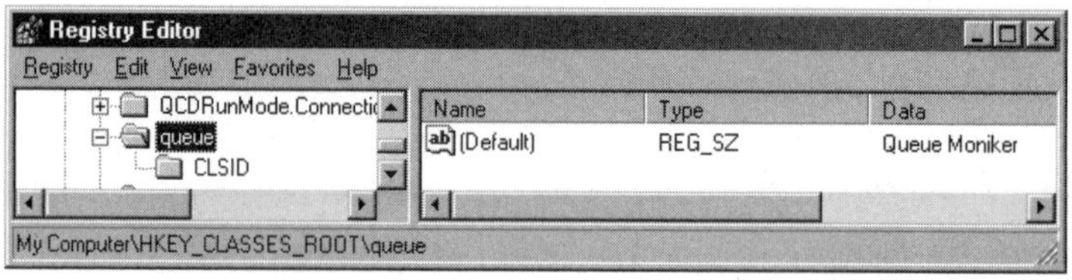

The queue moniker was added to the Microsoft Windows 2000 operating system for the purpose of creating a recorder object to simulate the presence of a queued component. *GetObject* creates an object of the queue-moniker class based on the supplied text string and tells the moniker to bind. It is up to the queue moniker to make sense of the string and return a recorder object having the correct properties and simulating the correct component. A full discussion of the moniker creation and binding process is beyond the scope of this book. A good explanation can be found in *Understanding ActiveX and OLE* by David Chappell (Microsoft Press, 1996).

The characters between "queue:" and the slash ("/") are used to supply options to the queue moniker. The preceding example doesn't contain any options, but other examples that use this feature will follow. The characters after the slash, in this case "new:VBShipProj.VBShip", are the initialization string for another type of moniker. This moniker is the *new* moniker, so called because it simulates the action of the *new* operator in many programming languages. This type of moniker creates a new COM object based on the ProgID that follows it. On the client side, the *new* moniker tells the queue moniker the class of object for which to records its calls. The *new* moniker is then serialized into a stream and transmitted to the server at the beginning of the bundle of recorded COM calls for this object. That's how the server knows which class of object to create in order to play back the calls.

The *new* moniker is also the mechanism by which you can create a component in both queued and nonqueued situations. To create a nonqueued component, just call *GetObject* without the queue moniker in front. The *new* moniker will properly create an instance of that class without the recorder intervening. Thus the statement would be as follows:

The *new* moniker is the mechanism by which you can create a component in both queued and nonqueued situations.

```
GetObject("new:VBShipProj.VBShip")
```

Since we are passing information to the queue moniker that tells it which class of object to record calls for, it makes sense that this should be the place where we pass to the recorder the specific MSMQ settings we want it to use. You change the default settings by passing additional data in the string used to initialize the queue moniker. For example, to create a *QC.Recorder* session that is aimed at a specific machine, you would say:

```
GetObject("queue:ComputerName=SomeMachine
    /new:VBShipProj.VBShip")
```

The attributes of MSMQ that are available to the QC developer are listed in Table 4-1. Some of these, such as the *Computer-Name* attribute shown above, are clearly useful to the application programmer. The utility of other attributes in the QC situation is less clear, primarily because many of them are used at a low level on the recipient server and not yet available to your actual component.

Table 4-1   MSMQ Attributes Available to Queued Components Through the Queue Moniker

Attribute	Meaning	Default Value
AppSpecific	Application-specific information which is attached to the message	None
AuthLevel	Specifies whether MSMQ authenticates its outgoing messages by attaching digital signatures to them	Derived from server application information installed on client
ComputerName	Name of computer on which recipient queue resides	Derived from server application information installed on client
Delivery	Specifies whether MSMQ messages are always committed to disk for reliability while in transit (recoverable) or kept in RAM for speed (express)	Recoverable

Attribute	Meaning	Default Value
Encrypt- Algorithm	Encryption algorithm used if sending a private message	MSMQ default
FormatName	Format name of the queue	MSMQ default
HashAlgorithm	Algorithm used for computing checksum to verify message hasn't been tampered with	MSMQ default
Journal	Specifies the journaling level of the queue	MSMQ default
Label	Human-readable string attached to a message	MSMQ default
MaxTimeTo- ReachQueue	Time after which message is deleted if it hasn't reached the queue on the recipient's machine	Infinite
MaxTime- ToReceive	Time after which message is deleted if it hasn't been read from the queue by the receiving application	Infinite
PathName	Full path name to the recipient queue	Derived from server application information installed on client
Priority	Priority level of sent messages, levels 1 through 7	MSMQ ignores priority for transacted queues
PrivLevel	Privacy level of message; determines whether message is encrypted or not	MSMQ default
QueueName	Name of destination queue on recipient machine	Derived from server application information installed on client
Trace	Specifies whether to generate response messages tracing a message's path through the MSMQ enterprise network	Off

Chapter Five

Events

Event Problem Background

Notifying interested parties of changes to data is a classic problem of distributed computing. One program detects a change in the world that it thinks other programs want to know about: a stock-ticker program notes a change in price, a weather monitoring program notes changes in barometric readings from remote sensors, a medical monitoring program notes that a patient's blood pressure has exceeded the acceptable range. Somewhere else in the world are other programs that would like to hear about changes such as these—a portfolio program that buys a stock when it hits a certain price, an alarm program that tells fishing boats to return to port, a patient monitoring program that signals the nurses' station that a patient requires medication.

The meanings of *client* and *server* become murky in discussions of scenarios like these, so I will introduce a new nomenclature for this chapter. Programs that provide notifications to other programs, for example the stock-ticker program, I will call *publishers*. Applications such as the portfolio program, which receive data from publishers and act on it, I will call *subscribers*.

A publisher detects a change that the subscriber cares about, but how does the subscriber find out from the publisher when a change takes place? The simplest approach is for the subscriber to poll the publisher every so often, analogous to you telephoning your stock-broker periodically to ask for the latest price of a stock. In the terminology of COM, the publisher would provide the subscriber

Notifying interested parties of changes to data is a classic problem of distributed computing.

Programs involved in event notification are called publishers and subscribers.

with an interface, and the subscriber would periodically call a method on that interface to see if any changes had taken place. (See Figure 5-1.)

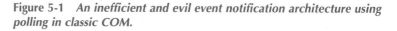

Figure 5-1   *An inefficient and evil event notification architecture using polling in classic COM.*

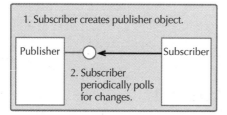

This strategy is simple to code, but it's a terrible idea for several reasons. First, the subscriber wastes an enormous amount of time and energy asking, "Are there any changes?" The publisher wastes another enormous amount of time and effort replying, "No, there aren't." You might just get away with polling in a desktop application that spends most of its time idling, waiting for user input, but it's deadly in an enterprise application where many clients connect to a single server. Mutual fund giant Fidelity recently announced restrictions on its account holders who phoned in too often. And anyone who has ever contemplated infanticide at the tenth repetition of "Are we almost there yet?" in as many minutes will understand the fundamental wrongness of this approach.

Polling is a terrible way for a subscriber to get data from a publisher.

Second, polling involves some inevitable amount of latency between the time the change occurs and the time the subscriber gets around to polling for it. On average, this latency is equal to half the polling interval. As you lengthen the polling interval to waste fewer CPU cycles, the latency increases. Not only is this latency bad in and of itself, but the fact that it is nondeterministic—that it varies from one occurrence to another—is also a problem in designing systems. Polling is evil in an enterprise application, so don't do it.

We would really like the publisher to initiate the notification process when it detects interesting changes in the world. Instead of you having to call your stockbroker periodically to find out the latest prices, it would save you both a lot of headaches if you gave your broker your phone number and asked him to call you when something changed. In COM terms, the subscriber provides the publisher with an interface, and the publisher calls a method on it when something interesting happens. This is the approach that ActiveX controls use to fire events to their containers, as shown in Figure 5-2. Here, the control is the publisher and the container is the subscriber.

Receiving a callback from the publisher, as with an ActiveX control event, is a much better notification scheme.

Figure 5-2 *The event notification architecture used by ActiveX controls.*

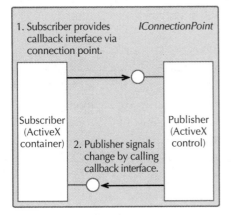

This type of event is called a *tightly coupled event.* The subscriber knows exactly which publisher to request notifications from (the container knows the CLSID, or class identifier, of the control) and the mechanism to be used to connect to it (the *IConnectionPointContainer* and *IConnectionPoint* interfaces exposed by the control). A tightly coupled event works reasonably well on a single desktop, but it has a number of drawbacks when it's used at the scale of an enterprise system.

Tightly coupled events pose problems for an enterprise system.

For the event mechanism to function, a tightly coupled event requires both the publisher and the subscriber to be running at all times. Both sides have to be running when the subscriber (container) provides the publisher (control) with its callback interface, and both sides have to be running when the publisher calls the notification method on the subscriber's interface. ActiveX controls are mostly used for desktop user interface elements, which have no reason not to match the lifetime of their containers, so this restriction is not usually a problem. However, requiring lifetimes to overlap can be a big problem in enterprise applications, as we saw in Chapter 4. We'd like the subscriber to be able to make subscription requests while the publisher isn't running, and we'd like the publisher to be able either to launch the subscriber just in time to fire an event or to use Queued Components instead of direct connections for sending event notifications, or both.

> Tightly coupled events require publisher and subscriber lifetimes to overlap.

The second problem with tightly coupled events is that the subscriber needs to know the exact mechanism a particular publisher requires for establishing subscriptions, and this mechanism can vary radically from one publisher to another. For example, ActiveX controls use the *IConnectionPoint* mechanism for hooking up the callback circuit to deliver notifications of their events. An OLE (object linking and embedding) server uses the method *Advise* on the *IOleObject* interface to hook up a callback circuit to deliver notifications of embedding-related events, and so on. We would really like to standardize one connection mechanism for publishers and subscribers. We would also like to be able to use this standard connection mechanism administratively, instead of having to write code to access it.

> Tightly coupled events require publisher and subscriber to have intimate knowledge of each other.

The third problem with the tightly coupled event mechanism is that it contains no mechanism for filtering or interception. When I tell my broker that I care about changes to stock prices, he doesn't call me with the change of any stock price anywhere in the world. Instead, I tell him which stocks I care about, usually those that I own or am thinking about buying. I might even tell him that I care only about certain movements—for example, if the price of my

> Tightly coupled events don't allow for filtering or interception.

favorite stock tops $150, because it's time to cash out. We'd like to have some mechanism whereby a subscriber could specify that it wanted to receive calls only if their parameters had certain values—for example, if the parameter designating the stock symbol matched one that we cared about, or if the parameter designating the price was greater than a certain value. And ideally, we'd like to be able to specify this information administratively as well.

One solution to these problems would be to store the information about matching publishers with subscribers externally instead of inside the programs themselves. The publisher would maintain an external database containing a list of the different events for which it knew how to send notifications. Subscribers could read this list and pick the events that they wanted to hear about. The publisher would also maintain some sort of subscription database, conceptually similar to a mailing list, of the CLSIDs of subscribers that wanted to hear about each event. Administrative tools or the subscriber programs themselves would know how to make entries in this subscription database. When the publisher wanted to fire an event, it would look in this database, find the CLSIDs of all the interested subscribers, create a new object of each interested class and call a method on that object. We would call such an event *loosely coupled* instead of tightly coupled because the information about which subscriber wanted to hear from which publisher would be maintained in a central database instead of being bound to the programs themselves.

Loosely coupled events are often a better fit for the enterprise.

This promising design approach has two snags. First, you'd have to develop and maintain the events and subscriptions database and write all the code for the publisher-side event-firing mechanism and the administrative tools as well. You'd have to sell a lot of units before this approach became cost effective, and enterprise applications generally have relatively low unit volume compared to desktop applications. Your time and money would be much better spent on your business logic instead of an event infrastructure.

Second, even if you did develop all this infrastructure, your subscription process would still be different from every other vendor's. Subscribers would have to know not only the specific techniques required to subscribe to your events, but also the different mechanisms required for every other publisher they ever want to hear from.

The infrastructure required for loosely coupled events is best inherited from the operating system.

What you'd really like is to inherit such a mechanism from the operating system. This way you'd have to write very little code, and every vendor's subscription process would be the same as everyone else's. Are you starting to see a pattern in this book?

Solution Architecture

The COM+ *Event service* is the operating system service that deals with the matching and connection of publishers and subscribers. Its architecture is shown in Figure 5-3.

The COM+ Event service provides a loosely coupled event infrastructure.

An event, in this terminology, represents a single call to a method on a COM interface, originated by a publisher, and delivered by the Event service to the correct subscriber or subscribers. A publisher is any program that makes the COM calls that initiate events, and a subscriber is a COM+ component that receives the COM

Figure 5-3 *The COM+ Event service architecture.*

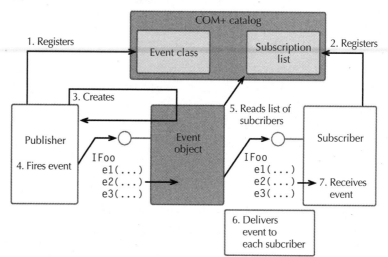

calls representing events from a publisher. The subscriber implements an interface as a COM server; the publisher makes calls on it as a COM client. The only change from classic COM is the Event service in the middle, which keeps track of which subscribers want to receive the calls and directs the calls to those subscribers without requiring the specific knowledge of the publisher.

Making a single event call is known as *firing* the event. You may also see the term *publishing* used in the documentation as a synonym for firing. This term suffers from ambiguity between its general meaning—to make information available—and its specific meaning—in this sense, to initiate a single event. Since *firing* is unambiguous, and is used in the names of the interfaces and methods relating to the event system, and is the term that the many, many users of ActiveX controls have used for over six years for similar actions, I will stick with it.

As shown in Figure 5-3, the connection between a publisher and a subscriber is represented by an *event class* (1). An event class is a COM+ component, *synthesized by the Event service*, that contains the interfaces and methods a publisher will call to fire events and that a subscriber needs to implement if it wants to receive events. The interfaces and methods provided by an event class are called *event interfaces* and *event methods*. You tell COM+ which interfaces and methods you want an event class to contain by providing COM+ with a type library. Event classes are stored in the COM+ catalog, placed there either by the publishers themselves or by administrative tools.

COM+ synthesizes an event class to represent a type of event that a publisher can fire.

A subscriber indicates its desire to receive events from a publisher by registering a *subscription* with the COM+ Event service (2). A subscription is a data structure that provides the Event service with information about the recipient of an event. It specifies which event class, and which interface or method within that event class, the subscriber wants to receive calls from. Subscriptions are stored in the COM+ catalog, placed there either by the subscribers themselves or by administrative tools. *Persistent* subscriptions survive a restart of the operating system; *transient* subscriptions do not.

Subscriber applications register their subscriptions with the COM+ catalog.

When a publisher
creates an object of an
event class and calls a
method, COM+'s Event
service locates and
notifies all the
subscribers.

When a publisher wants to fire an event, it uses the standard object creation functions, such as *CoCreateInstance* or *CreateObject*, to create an object of the desired event class (3). This object, known as an *event object*, contains the Event service's implementation of the requested interface. The publisher calls the event method that it wants to fire to the subscribers (4). Inside its synthesized implementation of the interface, the Event service looks in the COM+ catalog and finds all the subscribers to that interface and method (5). The Event service then connects to each subscriber (using any combination of direct creation, monikers, or queued components) and calls the specified method (6). The subscriber receives the incoming event notification on the event interface that it implements (7). Because frequently more than one subscriber wants notification for each event, event methods may not use output parameters and must return only success or failure *HRESULTs*—the same restrictions as for QC interface methods. Essentially any COM client can become a publisher and any COM+ component can become a subscriber. Neither has to know anything about the intervening gyrations performed by the Event service.

The current implementa-
tion of the Event service
has some limitations.

The current implementation of the Event service has some limitations. First, the subscription mechanism is not itself distributed. There is currently no enterprise-wide repository of all the publishers and subscribers. You could certainly construct one yourself by placing all the event classes and subscriptions on a central machine. Publishers would create event objects on the central machine, and subscribers receive their notifications from the Event service on that central machine. This approach would be easy to set up, but would cost you one extra network hop per event fired from the publisher—for the call to travel from the publisher's machine to the central machine. The central machine would also represent a single point of failure, so you'd have to back it up with a hot spare using Microsoft Clustering Services.

Second, delivery of events in the current system occurs either by DCOM or QC, which are one-to-one communication mechanisms. This means that the delivery time and effort increase linearly with the number of subscribers, which in turn means that the current system is not well suited to firing events to lots and lots of subscribers. The exact numbers of simultaneous subscribers that can be supported will obviously vary widely depending on system workload and hardware capacity, and in any event will have to await the final performance tuning of the product. For ballpark numbers at the time of this writing, figure that dozens of subscribers are probably fine, and thousands of subscribers are probably not fine. The current event system does not support broadcast datagrams, which would be the best way of reaching very large numbers of subscribers. If you need to, you can write one subscriber that receives events via DCOM and then resends the incoming data to many users via a datagram.

Simplest Event Example

The workings of the COM+ Event service are shown in the Publisher sample, a simulated stock-ticker program, available on this book's Web site. The Publisher sample application, shown in Figure 5-4, allows a human user to fire two events, one signaling a change in a stock price and the other signaling the listing of a new stock on the exchange. A sample subscriber is provided to demonstrate reception of calls from the event object. The combination shows the ease with which relatively simple programs that don't know anything about the COM+ Event service can nonetheless tap into its power by making simple administrative entries in the COM+ catalog.

An event workflow example begins here.

Figure 5-4   *The Publisher sample program.*

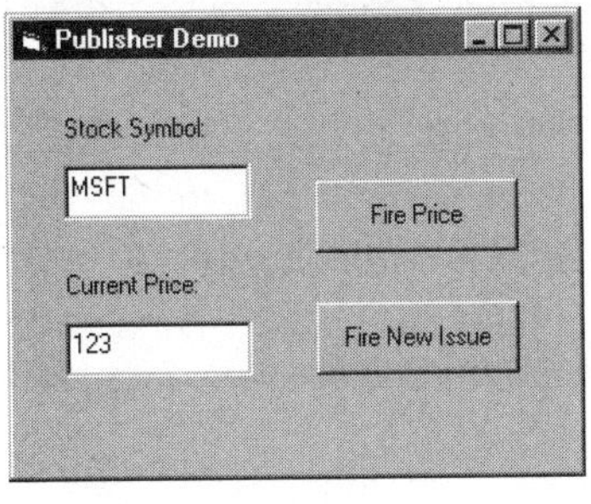

We first register event classes using the Component Services snap-in.

The first thing to do is register the event class. To do this, we need to create a new COM+ application and start installing a component by using the Component Services snap-in—clicking the Install New Event Class(es) button, as shown in Figure 5-5.[1]

Figure 5-5 ***Registering the event class using the Component Services snap-in.***

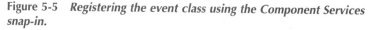

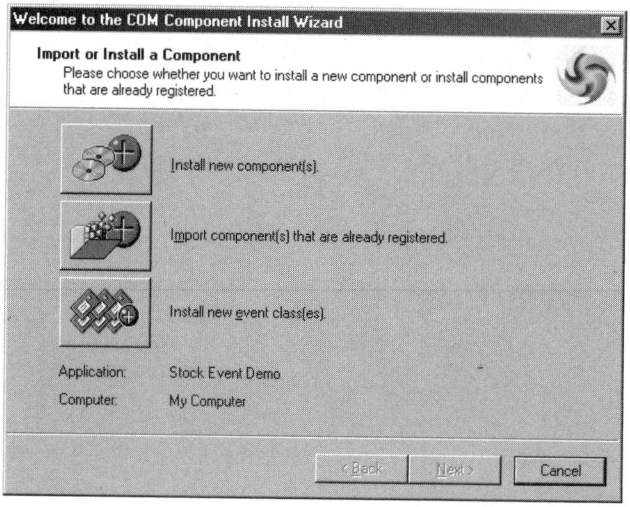

We need to provide COM+ with a type library describing the event interfaces and methods so that it will know how to synthesize the event class on our behalf. To work with the Event service, the type library needs to reside in or be accompanied by a self-registering DLL. The user interface used to make these settings is shown in Figure 5-6. I've registered the event class in the sample by using the ATL to create a dummy component called *StockEventCls*, (the name of the component and project can't be the same in the ATL) which you will find in the StockEventClass folder. It contains the definition of the interface that the subscriber will implement and that the publisher will call. In this case, the interface is named *IStockEventCls* and contains the

1. As we go to press, the event-related methods *GetEventClassesForIID*, *InstallEventClass*, and *InstallMultipleEventClasses* have been added to the *COMAdminCatalog* object methods listed in Table 2-1.

methods *StockPriceChanged* and *NewStockListed*. The Event service uses the type library and the self-registration code from this component. Even though I had to add implementations of the methods to the event class component because of the internal structure of the ATL, the methods on this component will never be called by the Event service. It was simply the fastest way to produce the type library and self registration that the Event service requires.

Figure 5-6 *The user interface for specifying the DLL containing the type library that describes the event class.*

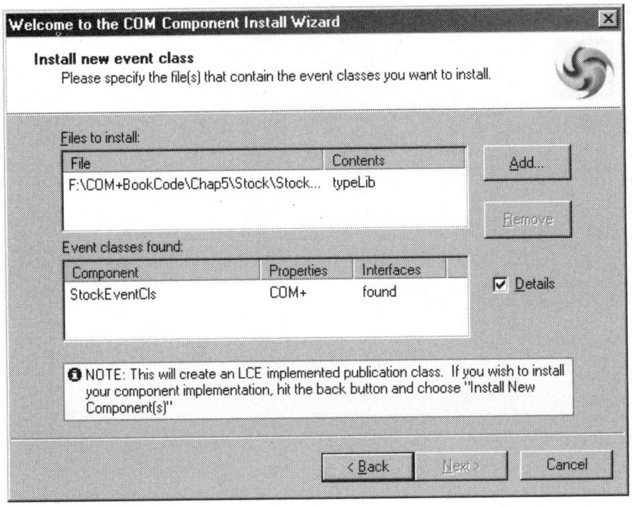

Entering the path to the event class component DLL and clicking OK tells the Component Services snap-in to synthesize an event class and install it in the COM+ catalog. The snap-in does this internally by going to the COM+ catalog (discussed in Chapter 2) and calling the method *ICOMAdminCatalog::InstallEventClass*. The component will look very much like any other component in the snap-in. The only discernible difference at this level is what's entered on the Advanced tab of the component's property sheet, as shown in Figure 5-7. In this example, I add a publisher ID

Entering the path to the event class component DLL and clicking OK tells the Component Services snap-in to synthesize an event class and install it in the COM+ catalog.

that will show up in the snap-in when I add the subscriptions to this event class later. This is all I need to do for a subscriber to find the event class and subscribe to it, and for a publisher to create an object of the event class and fire it.

Figure 5-7 *The event class component's Advanced properties tab.*

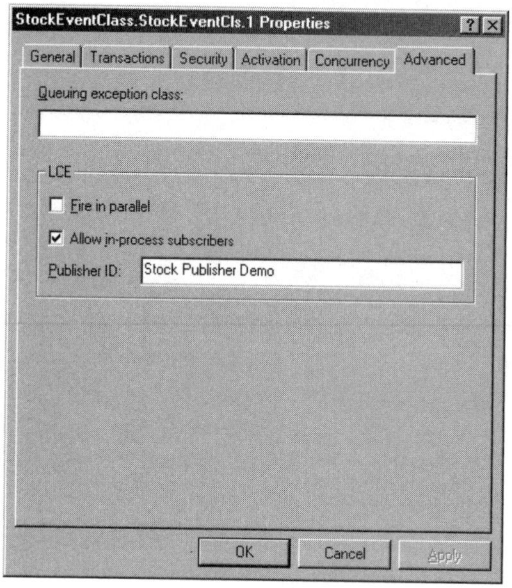

Next we add our subscriber, which must be a configured component in a COM+ application. You will find the subscriber component in the StockSubscriber folder. After you create an application and install the component as usual, you'll notice that each component shown in the snap-in contains a Subscriptions folder just beneath its Interface folder, as shown in Figure 5-8.

Next we register the subscriber component and add a subscription.

Right-clicking on the Subscriptions folder will bring up a wizard allowing you to enter a new subscription. The wizard will offer

Figure 5-8 *The Subscriptions folder in the Component Services snap-in.*

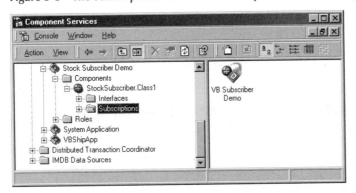

you a choice of all the interfaces that have been added as event classes, as shown in Figure 5-9.

Figure 5-9 *Using the New Subscription Wizard to select an available event class interface.*

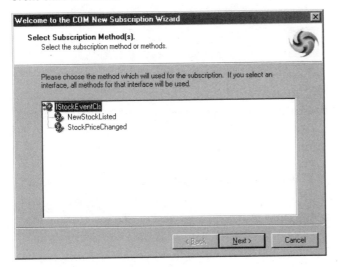

A single subscription can specify a single method or all methods on the interface. If you want to receive calls to more than one method but not every method, you must add a subscription for each desired method. The wizard searches the COM+ catalog for registered event classes that support the specified interface and offers you the choice to subscribe, as shown in Figure 5-10. You choose the publisher that you want your subscriber to hear from.

Figure 5-10   *Using the wizard to subscribe to an event class.*

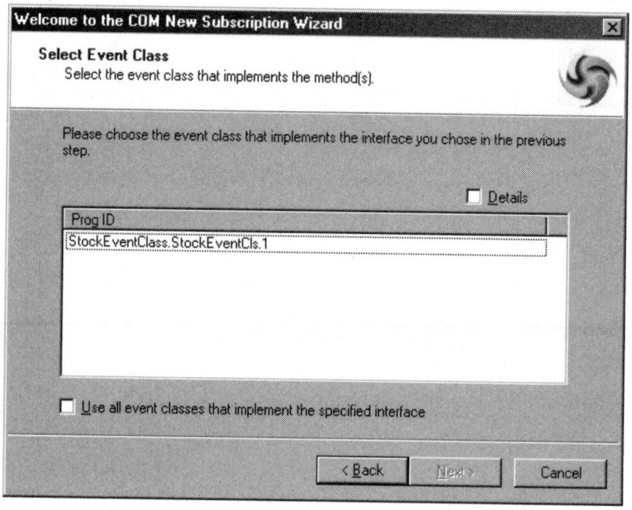

One additional step in the wizard, shown in Figure 5-11, allows you to enter a name for the subscription and, more important, enable the subscription. Subscriptions may be enabled or disabled. The latter receive no event notifications.

*That's all we have to do.
It's quite easy.*

That's all you have to do. When the Publisher application wants to fire an event, it simply creates an object of the event class and calls the method on it. The code to do this is identical to what the publisher would do if it was making calls on a single object in classic COM. The only difference is that the publisher creates an object of the COM+ synthesized event class instead of the subscriber class. When the publisher calls the method on the event class, the Event service looks through the COM+ catalog to find all the relevant subscribers. It creates the subscriber object in the manner specified by the subscriber—either directly, queued,

Figure 5-11 *The wizard step that will either enable or disable event notifications for the new subscription.*

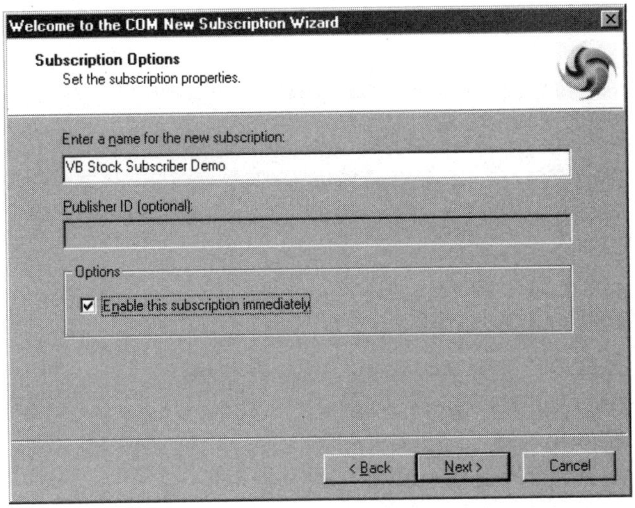

or with a moniker—and passes on to each of them the method call that the publisher originally made. A sample listing demonstrating this process is shown in Figure 5-12.

Figure 5-12 *A publisher firing an event.*

```
' Create the event class object

Dim foo As New StockEventCls

' Call the event class object's method that
' fires the StockPriceChanged event.

Private Sub Command1_Click()
 Call foo.StockPriceChanged(Text1.Text, CCur(Text2.Text))
End Sub

' Call the event class object's method that
' fires the NewStockListed event.

Private Sub Command2_Click()
 Call foo.NewStockListed(Text1.Text)
End Sub
```

The subscriber code is also quite similar to what it would be if it were called directly by the publisher instead of the event mechanism, as shown in Figure 5-13.

Figure 5-13   *A subscriber receiving an event notification.*

```
' The subscriber must implement the interface on
' which it wants to receive calls from the event object.

Implements StockEventCls

' Pop up message box telling user of
' NewStockListed event.

Private Sub StockEventCls_NewStockListed(ByVal Symbol _
  As String)
  MsgBox "New Stock " + Symbol + " has started trading", _
  vbOKOnly, "VB Event Subscriber"
End Sub

' Pop up message box telling user of
' StockPriceChanged event

Private Sub StockEventCls_StockPriceChanged(ByVal Symbol _
  As String, ByVal Price As Currency)
  MsgBox "The market price of stock " + Symbol + _
  " is now " + Str(Price), vbOKOnly, "VB Event Subscriber"
End Sub
```

That's all we have to do to tap into the COM+ Event service. We let go and let COM+.

More on Subscriptions

A subscription is a data structure that resides in the COM+ catalog. A subscription's properties are available through the *IEventSubscription* interface, shown in Table 5-1. Many of the properties can be modified through the Component Services snap-in, but others are not available through this user interface. You must write your own administrative utility program to access these properties.

Table 5-1 The *IEventSubscription* Interface Methods

Method	Description
SubscriptionID	Unique identifier for this subscription within the Event service.
SubscriptionName	Human-readable name for this subscription.
PublisherID	Unique identifier of publisher required by the subscription. If *NULL*, subscription accepts events from any publisher.
EventClassID	Exact event class that the subscription requires. Supported for backwards compatibility, generally ignored by subscribers in favor of *InterfaceID* property.
MethodName	Name of method from which subscriber wants to receive incoming event calls. Specified relative to *InterfaceID*.
SubscriberCLSID	COM+ component identifier of the subscriber. Used by event class to create the subscriber object.
SubscriberInterface	Actual *IUnknown* pointer to interface on which subscriber wants to receive incoming event calls. Used for transient subscriptions.
PerUser	When set to *TRUE*, the subscription only receives events when the user identified by the *OwnerSID* property is logged in.
OwnerSID	Security credential of program that creates a subscription.
Enabled	Turns on or off the delivery of events to the subscription.
Description	Unused by Event service. Available as a comment field for subscribers or administrators.
MachineName	Name of machine on which subscription resides.
PublisherProperty	A bag of properties set by subscriber. A publisher filter can examine the contents of the bag to decide whether to fire an event to the subscriber or to customize the information delivered to the subscriber.

(continued)

Table 5-1 *continued*

Method	Description
SubscriberProperty	Reserved for future use.
InterfaceID	Interface on which subscriber wants to receive incoming event notifications.
FilterCriteria	String used for filtering events at the event class. Calls whose parameters do not match the string are not forwarded to the subscriber.
Subsystem	Reserved for future use.
SubscriberMoniker	Moniker to use when activating a subscriber.

Subscriptions can be persistent or transient.

Subscriptions come in two flavors, *persistent* and *transient*. A persistent subscription is the type used in the Publisher sample. Persistent subscriptions live in the COM+ catalog and survive a system restart. They exist independently of the lifetime of the subscriber object. A subscriber program often creates a persistent subscription when the program is installed and removes the subscription when the program is uninstalled.

The COM+ Event service creates a new subscriber object each time it fires an event to a persistent subscriber.

When a publisher makes a call on an event object, the event object looks for all the persistent subscriptions in the catalog and creates a new instance of each subscriber class. The creation process can happen either directly or through a moniker (the latter being how queued components are used for event subscribers). You specify the subscriber object to create by setting the *SubscriberCLSID* or the *SubscriberMoniker* property of the subscription. The subscriber object created by a persistent subscription is always released after *each* event call, regardless of success or failure, and regardless of whether the publisher releases the event object. Any reader wanting to verify this can put a message box in the destructor (Microsoft Visual C++) or *Class_Terminate* (Microsoft Visual Basic) functions of the subscriber sample objects.

A transient subscription is a subscription that requests event calls be made to a specific existing subscriber object. Transient subscriptions are also stored in the COM+ catalog, but they do not survive a system shutdown. The Component Services snap-in has no provision for setting up transient subscriptions; it is up to the subscriber program to do that itself by using the COM+ administrative interfaces.

You set up a transient subscription by adding a new subscription to the Event service and setting its *SubscriberInterface* property to the *IUnknown* interface of the subscriber object. In this case, the event mechanism will not create a new instance of the subscriber object when firing an event, but it will use the one it has been handed. The Event service holds a reference count on the subscriber object until either an administrative program or the subscriber object itself removes it from the Event service.

COM+ maintains a reference count on the subscriber object provided with a transient subscription.

Because they do not involve repeated object creations and destructions, transient subscriptions are more efficient than persistent subscriptions, although they raise all the lifetime issues that persistent subscriptions abstract away. A transient subscription would be a good choice when a subscriber cared only about receiving updates during its own externally controlled lifetime. For example, an application that displayed the latest foreign exchange rates to a trader would care only about receiving updates when the trader was logged in. A persistent subscription would be a good choice when an application cared about any update but didn't want to hang out waiting for one to happen. For example, a financial arbitrage application might want to be launched only when spreads on exchange rates made it profitable.

Any subscription can be disabled. To do this, set the *Enabled* property of the subscription to *FALSE*. A disabled subscription is never called by the Event service.

Either type of subscription can be enabled or disabled.

More on Firing Events

All Event service operations have been completed by the time the publisher returns from calling an event method.

When an event method returns, everything that is going to happen on the publisher machine has already happened. All non-QC subscriber objects with transient subscriptions have been called and returned. All non-QC subscribers with persistent subscriptions have been created, called, returned, and released. Calls to all QC subscribers have been recorded, and the persistent ones enqueued for transmission. Since transient subscriber objects are not released until their subscriptions are removed, any transient QC subscriptions will not be enqueued until this happens.

A single result code tells the publisher the degree of success that firing the event accomplished.

The return code of an event method tells the publisher the result of the Event service's operation. The possible return codes are listed in Table 5-2. They tell the publisher that either all the subscribers returned success code S_OK, that some of them did, that none of them did, or that there weren't any subscribers. Currently there is no way at this level to determine which of the subscribers failed or for what reason. The design philosophy of loosely coupled events is that the publisher doesn't know or care who the different subscribers are. A publisher that can't live without this information can obtain it by implementing a publisher filter, as described later in this chapter.

The Event service also does not currently provide a simple mechanism for specifying the order in which an event is delivered to multiple subscribers. The default firing protocol is to fire events one at a

Table 5-2   Event Method Return Codes

Return Code	Meaning
S_SUCCESS	An event was able to invoke all of the subscribers.
EVENT_S_SOME_ SUBSCRIBERS_FAILED	An event was able to invoke some but not all of the subscribers.
EVENT_E_ALL_ SUBSCRIBERS_FAILED	An event was unable to invoke any of the subscribers.
EVENT_S_ NOSUBSCRIBERS	An event was published but there were no subscribers.

time, but in no deterministic or repeatable order. In this case as well, a publisher that needs to control the order in which subscribers receive an event can implement a publisher filter.

A publisher can mark an event for firing *in parallel* by selecting the Fire In Parallel check box shown previously in Figure 5-7. This allows the Event service to use multiple threads to deliver an event to more than one subscriber at a time. This can greatly decrease the average delivery time of event notifications in certain circumstances. For example, suppose the first subscriber to an event took a long time to process an event notification, perhaps having to block while waiting for something else in the system to complete processing. Without firing in parallel, all the other subscribers to the event would have to wait for the first subscriber to finish before receiving their event notifications. If firing in parallel is enabled, other threads could be firing the events to the other subscribers, bypassing the blocked one. Selecting this check box only allows parallel delivery, it doesn't guarantee it.

The Event service does not provide a mechanism for administratively specifying the order in which subscribers are notified of an event.

Subscriber Parameter Filtering of Incoming Calls

You saw how easy it is to hook up a subscriber to be notified when a publisher fires an event. At times it's too easy. A subscriber might not care about everything a publisher has to say. For example, most investors are probably interested in changes in the prices of only a small subset of stocks traded worldwide, those that an investor owns or is considering buying. We could certainly write code on the subscriber side to check the incoming stock symbol and ignore it if it isn't one of the ones we care about, but doing this is inefficient on two counts. First, it wastes a lot of CPU time by rejecting an incoming event call late in the event process—the Event service would have already created the subscriber object and made the call into it. It makes sense to have that check and possible rejection occur as far upstream as possible so that we don't waste time on a useless operation. Second, it requires writing code on the subscriber to filter the event, and we'd really like to avoid that, if possible, by handling the task administratively.

The ability to filter incoming event calls can increase system efficiency.

The Event service provides an administrative way of filtering event calls based on parameter values.

The COM+ Event service provides this capability by allowing a subscriber to specify a *filter-criteria string* as part of its subscription. The user interface for doing this is shown in Figure 5-14. You specify the criteria to be met by using the variable names specified in the type library. The Event service then evaluates the variables at call time and allows the call to proceed only if the criteria in the string evaluate to *TRUE*. Figure 5-14 shows a filter string that will result in the specified event being fired only for changes to stocks in which the variable named *Symbol* has the string value "MSFT". The filter-criteria string recognizes standard relational operators ($<$, $>$, $=$, and so on), nested parentheses, and logical keywords AND, OR, and NOT. For example, the following string would be understood:

```
(Symbol = "IBM" AND Price > 200) OR
(Symbol = "MSFT" AND Price < 150)
```

Figure 5-14 *The user interface for specifying filtering criteria for a subscription.*

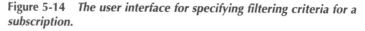

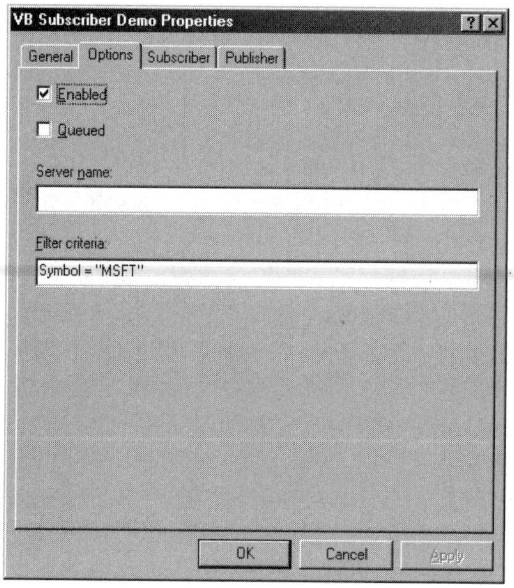

Publisher Filtering of Outgoing Calls

The example shown earlier in this chapter demonstrated the simplest way of getting the job done. It completely let go and let COM+, an approach that makes it extremely easy to write and deploy applications, but may not always be as flexible as you need. In particular, the system as demonstrated offers no possibility of controlling the order in which subscribers receive their events, nor does it offer any chance for the publisher to refuse to deliver an event to a specific subscriber. These types of decisions are often part of a publisher's business logic. For example, a publisher might want to check its current financial records to see if a subscriber has paid the requisite fees before actually firing an event. For another example, the publisher might want to fire events to subscribers in a particular order; perhaps some subscribers have paid extra for priority notification. The default functionality of the Event service does not handle these situations. For maximum flexibility, we need a way for the publisher to inject itself into the Event service's logic at event firing time.

We would sometimes like a greater degree of control over the event system than the automatic mechanism permits administratively.

The publisher can exercise fine-grained control over the event firing process by means of the *IEventControl* interface, whose methods are listed in Table 5-3. Of particular interest is the method *GetSubscriptions*, which returns an enumerator object that the publisher can use to examine the subscribers for the event and determine whether to fire it and in which order the subscribers should receive notification. The collection is self-updating—every time you walk it you get the current list of subscribers, with additions and removals being taken into account.

A publisher can access the *IEventControl* interface by querying the event object. However, accessing it at this point raises several problems. First, it won't work if the event class itself is a queued component. This is an entirely reasonable design, as discussed in the next section. The interface isn't queueable because it contains output parameters. (See Chapter 4.) Second, this strategy works only if it is compiled into the publisher program. It won't help you control a publisher that you bought from a third party or obtained from another part of your company to which you don't have the source code. If you use this approach, you won't be able to change your filter behavior without rebuilding your entire publisher program. We'd like our publisher control mechanism to work with QC and to work without requiring modification of the publisher code.

Table 5-3   The *IEventControl* Interface Methods

Method	Description
SetPublisherFilter	Allows publisher to specify desired filter class at runtime rather than at registration time
AllowInprocActivation	Allows publisher to override administrative in-proc activation setting at runtime
GetSubscriptions	Returns self-updating collection of subscriptions to specified method
SetDefaultQuery	Sets filter criteria to use on specified method when publisher filter is not installed

We can attain this greater degree of control by writing a publisher filter.

Fortunately, the COM+ Event service provides a *publisher filter* mechanism that allows us to handle these cases. A publisher filter is a COM+ component that is installed downstream of the event object, as shown in Figure 5-15. Putting our publisher modification code in a publisher filter means that it will work both with QC and with third-party software. Use of the publisher filter is shown in Figure 5-16. You tell COM+ which publisher filter to use for an event class by setting the event class's *PublisherFilterCLSID* property in the COM+ catalog. The Component Services snap-in contains no user interface for this; you will have to write your own administrative application to do it.

Figure 5-15   *Position of a publisher filter.*

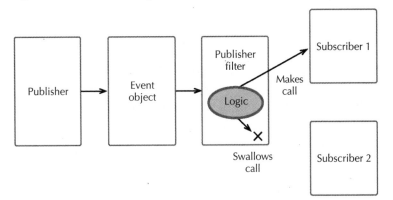

Figure 5-16   *Control flow through a publisher filter.*

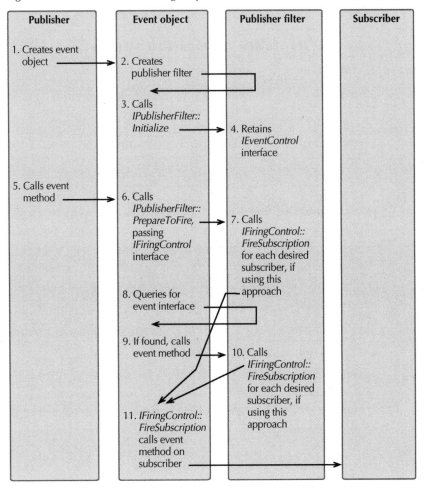

The Event service creates
the filter object when the
publisher creates the
event object.

When the publisher creates the event object (1), the Event service reads the CLSID of the filter specified for that event class and creates an object of the filter class (2). If the filter object cannot be created, the creation of the event object fails. The filter class must implement the *IPublisherFilter* interface, whose methods are shown in Table 5-4. If the event class supports more than one interface, the publisher filter must support the *IMultiInterface-PublisherFilter* interface instead. The *IMultiInterfaceEventControl* and *IMultiInterfacePublisherFilter* interfaces supersede *IEventControl* and *IPublisherFilter*. You are encouraged to implement *IMultiInterfaceEventControl* and *IMultiInterfacePublisherFilter* for composition with QC and for handling multiple interfaces on an event class. In this book however, I will discuss only the *IPublisherFilter* interface for simplicity.

Table 5-4   The *IPublisherFilter* Interface Methods

Method	Description
Initialize	Called by the Event service when the filter object is first created. Passes *IEventControl* for filter to use.
PrepareToFire	Called by Event service to tell filter object to examine its collection of subscriptions and fire the ones that it decides should be fired.

After creating the filter object, the Event service will call the *IPublisherFilter::Initialize* method, passing an *IDispatch* interface, which you query for the *IEventControl* interface (3) or *IMultiInterfaceEventControl,* if filtering more than one interface (not shown). This interface is only passed once, here in the *Initialize* method, so if you want to use it later, you have to hang on to it here (4).

When the publisher calls a method on the event interface exposed by the event object (5), the Event service will call the filter's *IPublisherFilter::PrepareToFire* method (6). The first parameter specifies the name of the method to be fired, the second is an interface pointer of type *IFiringControl*. This interface has one method, *FireSubscription*. You use it to tell the Event service to deliver events to one subscriber. Calling this method invokes all of the Event service's standard delivery mechanisms, which include the parameter filtering described in the previous section (jump ahead to step 11).

At this point, you have two choices. If all your filter wants to do is use its business logic to swallow calls to certain recipients, your filter need not support the actual event interface that the publisher is calling; it need only support *IPublisherFilter*. You can write in your filter some mechanism for checking which subscribers are supposed to receive the event and which are not. Within the *PrepareToFire* method, you call *IFiringControl::FireSubscription* for every subscription in the list that you want to deliver (7).

The publisher filter can specify the order in which subscribers are called and even swallow calls to undesired subscribers.

You might, however, want your filter to perform more sophisticated logic based not just on the subscriber list but also on the parameters passed by the publisher to this individual method. For example, you might want to deliver a stock price change event to George only if the new stock price is at least $5 above the cost of his current holdings of that stock, which the publisher knows as part of its business logic. To perform filtering at this level, your filter class must support the event interface that it is filtering, in addition to *IPublisherFilter*. After calling *PrepareToFire*, the Event service will query for this interface (8). If it finds it, the Event service will then call the actual event method on your filter object (9). Within this method, you will look at the parameters, decide which subscribers you want to receive the event, and call *FireSubscription* for each of them (10).

The filter mechanism can examine the event method parameters in order to help make its decision.

Events and Queued Components

Events and QC solve different problems. Events exist to handle the question of which publisher talks to which subscriber. The COM+ event mechanism tracks the desired delivery paths administratively, which saves you a lot of development time. QC, on the other hand, exists to asynchronously transfer COM calls from

Events and QC were designed to work well together.

client to object. The QC mechanism keeps you from having to match the lifetimes of client and server, which again saves you a lot of development time. Events would be much less useful if they required all parties to an event delivery to be running at the same time. Fortunately, events and QC were designed to work well together, and the combination can be quite powerful.

An example using events and QC begins here.

QC and events can be combined in two different ways, which can work simultaneously if you want. Consider the following problem: A nurse carries her handheld PC on her evening rounds of patient rooms and discovers that a patient has died in bed. She makes an entry to that effect in the patient chart program running on her handheld PC. There are a number of other programs in the hospital enterprise that might want to know about the patient's death—the finance department to prepare the final bill, the food service to check what they had last fed the poor devil, and the undertaker running Microsoft Morgue to come collect the body. You do not want the knowledge of which other programs need to hear about the patient's death to reside in the patient chart program; you do not want the patient death event to be tightly coupled to its subscribers. What would happen, for example, when a new application came online that also wanted to hear about patients' deaths, say Microsoft Chaplain? (Buy indulgences over the Web with our new secure e-commerce! OK, at least the Lutherans thought that was funny.) You would have to rewrite the patient chart program and every other publisher in the enterprise. Not a good idea.

COM+'s loosely coupled events are a natural for this situation. Every program that wants to hear about a patient death would make a subscription entry in the COM+ catalog. The publisher would then create a single event object and call a method on it. Keeping track of, locating, and delivering the event to all the registered subscribers is then the problem of the COM+ Event service. We don't have to write any code for it; we just inherit the functionality from the operating system.

Chapter Five

That's great, except that the different lifetimes and different connection times of the different programs in the enterprise mean that synchronous DCOM just will not work to connect them. The odds that all the machines containing interested programs are running and connected to the network at the same time are vanishingly small. Using QC abstracts away the lifetime problem quite nicely; that's what it's for. But we somehow have to tie it to the Event service. The nurse's handheld PC application needs to be able to fire an event while disconnected, recording it for playback later when she reconnects to the main network. Subscribers also need to be able to receive their event notifications when they come on line.

Both of these situations are quite easy to handle with QC. You handle the first case, firing the event while the nurse is disconnected, by placing the event class on a central server machine and by making the event class itself a queued component. It's a trivial matter: simply select the Queued check box shown previously in Figure 5-14, just as you would for any other component. The nurse's patient chart program will create the event object using a queue moniker, which means it will be connected to the QC recorder instead of to the actual event object, as described in Chapter 4. The calls that it makes to the event interfaces will be recorded for later playback. When the nurse reconnects to the network at the end of her rounds, the recorded calls to the event class will be forwarded and replayed on the main event machine and the event fired to its subscribers at that time.

An event class may be a queued component.

Why did we put the event class on a central server machine instead of directly on the nurse's handheld PC? Because in version 1.0 of the COM+ Event service, subscriptions are machine-specific. A subscriber can't just say that it wants to hear news about patient deaths from anyone on the network who ever sends it. By putting the event class on a central server machine, subscribers can subscribe to it there and know that all publishers will be using it to fire the events. Since this machine would then become the hub of your entire enterprise notification system, you would definitely want to provide a hot spare or two via clustering services to ensure you didn't have a single point of failure.

Event subscribers can also be queued components.

What happens if any of the subscribers aren't running when the event class does get fired? It's simple: use QC for them too. When you mark the subscriber interface as queued, as shown in Chapter 4, simply set up a subscription to an event class as we did earlier. When the publisher creates the event object and calls the event method, the event object will create a queued connection to the subscriber object and deliver its event notification that way.

What hazards or pitfalls are there to using QC in an event situation? The main one involves the order in which events are delivered. Remember that QC records and plays back all of the calls within the lifetime of a single object in a single MSMQ message. All calls made to a single QC object are guaranteed to be replayed in the order in which they were made. However, the results of more than one QC session with more than one object are not guaranteed to be replayed in the order in which the sessions occurred. This can cause trouble if the two sessions are related in an order-dependent manner.

Using events and QC together requires careful thought about the order in which events need to be received.

For example, suppose a publisher creates queued event object A, makes a few calls on it, and releases it. A single MSMQ message gets sent to the server containing all the calls made to object A. The same publisher now creates queued event object B in the same COM+ application, makes calls on it, and releases it. A single MSMQ message gets sent to the server containing all the calls made to object B. MSMQ works on a FIFO basis, so you know that the message carrying object A's calls will get dequeued before the message carrying object B's calls. However, the QC listener uses multiple threads to increase its throughput. The message carrying object B's calls can easily be dequeued on a thread different from the message carrying object A's calls, and essentially anything in the operating system can affect the scheduling of different threads. Perhaps the calls to object A need to wait on some external object during playback, but the calls to object B don't. You have no way of necessarily knowing that the calls made on one queued event object will or will not be played back before the calls made on a different queued object. Any sort of time dependence is anathema to QC. And except for the case of calls to a single object, so is any kind of order dependence. If it is important to you that one event necessarily take place before another, you have to make the calls on the same specific QC object instance or provide some sort of outside application logic that enforces the desired order.

In the hospital scenario, for example, suppose you have one event that announces the death of a patient and another that announces that a patient has been transferred to a certain bed. If you send out the death event first, and ten minutes later send the event that announces that a live patient has been transferred to the same bed, there is no way of guaranteeing that the death event will be processed first on every subscriber. A doctor's computer might actually process the events in an order which says, "There's a new patient in bed 330," and then "The patient in bed 330 just died," leading to a scene reminiscent of Monty Python and the Holy Grail (Pt: "I'm not dead!"; Dr: "Yes, you are"; Pt: "I think I'll go for a walk"; Dr: "You're not fooling anybody"). To avoid this kind of trouble and its resulting lawsuits, you need to design your system in such a manner that events are self-contained—they carry with them all the information needed to get the job done. In this example, the events depended on each other. Remember college chemistry labs when you didn't label your test tubes but just remembered the order in which you had placed them in the rack? A better design would be to have each event carry patient identification data so that the doctor would at least know which patient had died.

Events and Transactions

As we have seen throughout this book, transactions are a very useful feature. Any service that doesn't work and play well with transactions has a very limited future in the enterprise. Accordingly, the COM+ Event service is compatible with transactions. If

Events can work and play well with transactions.

a publisher is participating in a transaction, you can arrange for the transaction to be propagated to the subscribers so that they can vote on its outcome.

For example, consider the case of business rules. Suppose you have a publisher that wants to make some updates to a database. Suppose you also have a set of business rules to guard the integrity of your database. These business rules can easily vary from one location to another—for example, when different states impose different regulatory requirements. The publisher does not want the burden of keeping track of all the rules; it's much more cost effective if that's an administrator's job. The publisher just needs to work correctly with whichever rules exist in a particular installation.

Rather than write the publisher application to keep track of all the different business rules that apply in a particular situation, it would be very convenient to create a business rule event that a publisher would fire within the context of a transaction. An administrator would install subscriptions for all the business rules that the publisher needed to apply. You could use filtering to avoid wasting time on useless calls; for example, if the patient's age is less than 65, don't check the Medicare rules. The business rule subscribers would abort the transaction if any of their strictures were violated.

A publisher's transaction can be propagated to the event class and thence to the subscribers.

You do this by simply setting the event class and the subscriber components to support transactions, using the Component Services snap-in or the other mechanisms shown previously in Chapter 3. The publisher's transaction will be propagated to the event class and thence to the subscribers. The subscribers can use the *IObject-Context* interface to vote to commit or abort the transaction.

A problem can arise with multiple deliveries of events if some of the subscribers are transacted and some are not. Suppose a publisher, within the context of a transaction, fires an event. A transacted subscriber uses resource managers to make changes to a database, and then another transacted subscriber aborts the transaction. The publisher's changes and the first subscriber's changes will be rolled back as the transaction aborts. So far so good. But what happens if a nontransacted third subscriber has made persistent changes to a resource, perhaps to a plain old flat file (remember them)? When the publisher retries the transaction, all the transacted resources will be starting from their original state because they threw away their changes when the first transaction aborted. The nontransacted subscriber, however, will not know that the transaction aborted, so it will not have rolled back its state. Beware of mixing transacted and nontransacted subscribers into the same event.

Event Security

The Event service has the same security considerations as any other portion of COM+. The standard security mechanisms used in the other portions of COM+ apply to events as well, and function in the same way.

Security for installing an event class is the same as for installing any other component. Only members of the COM+ system application's Administrators role are allowed to do it. In addition, you want to ensure that a malicious subscriber doesn't add millions of subscriptions to deliberately gum up the works, and also that no unauthorized user is even allowed to read the subscription database. These actions, too, are restricted to members of the Administrators role.

Event subscribers may need to authenticate the identity of their publisher, to ensure that the organization offering them such a good rate on their foreign exchange transactions really is the bank that it claims to be. Subscriber applications do this by using the COM+ authentication mechanism, described in Chapter 2, in exactly the same manner as any other application.

> Event system security uses the same security mechanisms employed by the other parts of COM+.

> Event subscriber components perform authorization using the same role-based mechanism as any other component.

An event subscriber may be configured as a COM+ server application running in a separate process from the publisher or as a library application sharing the same process. Remember that components sharing the same process share the same address space and can thus read and write any portion of each other's memory. Also, components sharing the same process run with the identity of the same security principal, unless they go out of their way to change it. Any outgoing calls made by the in-proc component will have the identity of the client process.

The relationship between publisher and subscriber is usually less familiar and trusting than relationships between components in other places in COM+. Remember that the design philosophy of loosely coupled events means that the publisher often doesn't know or care who is subscribing to its events. The publisher can trust the security mechanism to ensure that no subscriber is allowed access who shouldn't receive the information the publisher is sending with its events, but it's a long way from there to feeling comfortable allowing the subscriber into the publisher's address space.

If the event class and subscriber component are both configured as library applications, the subscriber object could be created in the publisher's address space. A publisher probably doesn't want that, unless you know exactly who all the subscribers are and trust them all not to hurt you—a level of trust unusual in the real enterprise, although not unheard of. If the publisher wants to allow subscribers configured in library applications to share its address space, it selects the Allow In-Process Subscribers check box shown previously in Figure 5-7. If this check box is not selected, the subscriber object will be created in a separate process, even if it is configured to run as a library application.

Chapter Six

In-Memory
Database

Data Caching Problem Background

The primary goal of most enterprise systems is to provide easy, secure access to data that resides in databases. A travel agent needs to know flight availability, a stockbroker needs to see current stock prices, an author who's sent a manuscript to a publisher needs to find out where it currently is. Every client wants to see the data as quickly as possible—the stockbroker could lose his shirt on a five-minute delay, and the author, her patience. To avoid bottlenecks, a server that handles a large volume of requests needs to process each one as quickly as possible.

Enterprise applications need to provide fast access to databases.

The single best speed optimization technique in all of computing is to put code and data into fast silicon RAM instead of onto a slow iron disk. As you ponder the cost difference between a 450-MHz and a 500-MHz processor and wonder whether the added 11 percent raw speed improvement is worth the extra money, consider that accessing silicon is something like 1000 times faster (100,000 percent) than accessing iron. Until you've gotten everything possible off the iron and into silicon, any other design tweaks aimed at increasing speed pale into best-forgotten insignificance. Until your machine can't hold any more, your performance money is best spent on silicon RAM.

Accessing silicon RAM is about 1000 times faster than accessing iron disks.

We could greatly increase system throughput by caching frequently read data in RAM.

Most programmers think of databases as providing durability of data, which is a major concern in transaction processing. (See Chapter 3.) However, the database access provided by many enterprise applications consists almost entirely of reads. Think about stock-quote Web sites or the Victoria's Secret online catalog. The programs that read these databases spend an awful lot of time waiting for an iron disk to crawl around to the sector they actually care about. We could really enhance the throughput of these applications if we moved the databases they are reading from slow iron into fast silicon. While writing to these databases would still require moving iron to make the data durable, this happens so seldom compared with reading that it wouldn't matter.

Improving performance depends on identifying and deploying the database elements that should reside in main memory.

It's a great concept. RAM is cheap today, about $3 per megabyte at the time of this writing, less in quantity. One gigabyte (GB) of RAM would cost between $2500 and $3000, well within the budget constraints for any type of enterprise server project. The difficulty arises in specifying how the operating system is to use these large amounts of RAM: How do we reserve RAM for the use of our database instead of for other parts of the operating system? How do we specify which portions of which databases live in it? How do we do all this at an administrative level without requiring programmers? The $3000 we'd spend on RAM won't even buy two geek-weeks of programmer time.

Further performance increases are possible by caching frequently accessed data on the middle-tier machine.

Once we've gotten the database off the disk and into memory, we still have the problem of network latency. In three-tier systems, a network jump often separates the business-logic middle tier from the back-end database tier. While still much faster than moving iron, this network jump can also present a performance bottleneck, especially on the Internet. It would be great if we could find some way to cache frequently accessed data on the middle-tier machine, especially if the data could be made to reside in the same process as the business logic. Again, this doesn't help us when we are writing to a database, but for many applications, reads vastly outnumber writes.

Once we start moving databases into RAM, we have to worry about running out of address space in our process. The Win32 flat memory model has hitherto provided only 2 GB of address space for our application, the rest being reserved for the operating system. We'd like a way to get more today, if possible. And we'd also like it if our database solution would transparently support 64-bit memory addressing when the operating system provides it.

Increasing RAM caching leads to increased need for address space.

If we did all these things, not only would our classic read-mostly databases speed up enormously, but using a database might become fast enough and easy enough to be cost-effective in software designs that employ structures such as large arrays or lists. We could use a database for transient state management among objects. In certain applications, we wouldn't even care if the database was backed by an underlying persistent data store—in fact, we'd just as soon turn that off. We'd just use the database for easy-to-program, very fast access to transient data. While you don't usually think of solving these problems by using a database, the savings in development time might be significant.

An automatic database memory caching system would be a great thing, so the only question is whether to write our own or inherit one from the operating system. Where have you seen this question before, and what was the answer then? We can inherit a rich database caching scheme if we let go and let COM+.

Solution Architecture

COM+'s In-Memory Database (IMDB) service is the mechanism that permits frequently used database elements to reside transparently in main memory caches within its middle-tier client's process, thereby greatly increasing the speed of reading the data. The architecture of a typical IMDB node is shown in Figure 6-1.

COM+'s IMDB service is used to improve performance by caching data on the middle-tier client.

A base client application has no knowledge of IMDB; it simply accesses the middle tier in its standard way. The base client might use DCOM to create a middle-tier COM+ object that accesses

Figure 6-1 *IMDB architecture.*

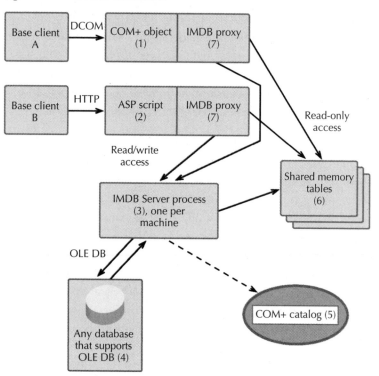

IMDB (1), or it might use HTTP to view an ASP page containing a middle-tier COM+ object that accesses IMDB (2).

The IMDB Server is the heart of IMDB.

Every middle-tier machine runs a single process called the *IMDB Server* (3) as a system service. This server is the center of all IMDB activity on the machine. The IMDB Server communicates by means of OLE DB with all the databases for which it provides caching (4). OLE DB is a low-level COM-based data access architecture that allows any application to expose its internal data through a standardized set of interfaces. For more information on OLE DB, see the articles by Stephen Rauch in the July 1996 and September 1997 issues of *Microsoft Systems Journal*.

When the IMDB Server starts up, it consults the COM+ catalog (5) to see which tables from which data sources it has been told to cache. These catalog entries are made by the system administrator, as described in more detail in the following section. The server reads and uses most configuration information on startup, so if the server is already running when IMDB configuration changes are made, it must be stopped and restarted for the changes to take effect. A table can be configured to load at startup or to load dynamically when requested by a client. The current version of IMDB contains no provision for dynamically unloading a table, nor does it provide any way to cache a subset of records in a table. The IMDB Server loads these tables into shared memory, which will be mapped into every process that needs to access it (6). The IMDB Server also allows IMDB clients to create database tables that are not backed by any underlying database. These tables are used for fast access to transient data, such as state shared among transactional components.

> The IMDB Server places database cache tables on the machine and in the address space of its clients.

IMDB exposes an OLE DB interface to its middle-tier clients, whom I will call *IMDB clients* to distinguish them from the client-tier base clients. Although you might see what I call IMDB clients referred to as *client components* in some of the documentation, I find that term ambiguous. The IMDB client can access IMDB's OLE DB interface directly or through the intermediation of an ADO object. An OLE DB object runs faster, but ADO is easier to program, so it usually ships faster.

> Clients access IMDB tables with OLE DB or ADO.

When the IMDB client opens its connection to the database, the IMDB Server provides it with an *IMDB proxy* object (7). This is a COM+ object provided by the operating system. The IMDB proxy lives in the IMDB client's address space, which makes accessing the proxy very fast. The IMDB proxy is smart. It knows that read operations should be fetched directly from the shared memory tables, as shown in Figure 6-1. It also knows that write operations need to go back to the IMDB Server, to be propagated to the back-end database if necessary. The IMDB proxy DLL uses

Microsoft Windows 2000's fast Local Procedure Call (LPC) facility to implement the quickest interprocess communication with the IMDB Server.

COM+ provides transaction services to ensure correctness of IMDB updates.

COM+ provides the transaction semantics and the automatic enlistment in the distributed transaction coordinator (DTC) to provide correctness for data updates from multiple IMDB clients to the underlying database.

Simplest IMDB Example

An IMDB example begins here.

Let's look at a sample enterprise application that uses IMDB. The IMDB sample (IMDBSamp1) demonstrates how an active server page running in Microsoft Internet Information Server (IIS) can read data from the IMDB and return it to an HTML client, in this case Microsoft Internet Explorer. The sample code is available on this book's Web site.

Using IMDB is primarily an administrative process.

Using IMDB is primarily an administrative operation, not a programming task, so you may find the setup a bit complicated. Follow the directions in the sample carefully if you want it to work. On the other hand, the programming is fairly easy and very similar to any other database programming that you've ever done.

The IMDB Server must be running.

The administrator must first configure IMDB on the server machine. This requires manipulation of the COM+ catalog, which I discussed in Chapter 2 and have used in every example since. The first thing to do is to launch the IMDB Server, and the easiest way to do this is by right-clicking on My Computer in the Component Services snap-in and choosing Start IMDB. You can also use the system service administrative tools to ensure that this service always starts when the system boots, as shown in Figure 6-2. The Task Manager in Figure 6-3 shows that IMDBSRV.EXE is running, which means that this step has been successful.

There are a number of administrative settings that configure operation of IMDB.

There are a number of administrative settings that tailor the performance of the IMDB Server process. The user interface for changing them is shown in Figure 6-4 on page 192. The Load Tables Dynamically check box specifies whether the IMDB Server should wait for a client to request a table before loading it or should load all of the tables for all of its data sources when the process starts. There is currently no provision for loading some tables at startup and others on demand. You can also specify the total amount of system memory available to IMDB. The Cache BLOB (binary large object) Size setting (which is not relevant to this example) is discussed later in this chapter. If you set either of the last two values to *0*, as shown, the system will use reasonable default values.

Figure 6-2   *The system service manager showing IMDB Server.*

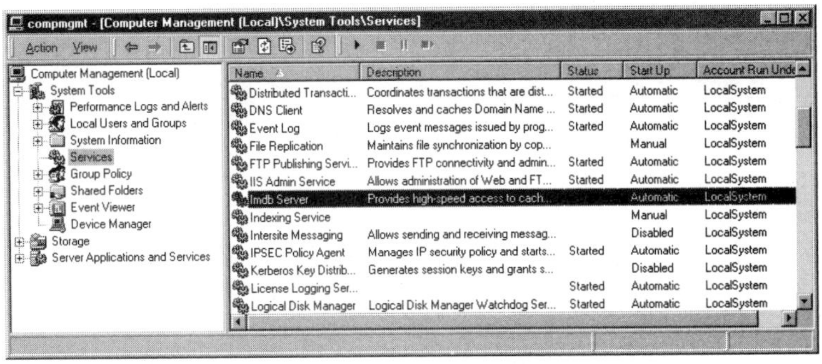

Figure 6-3   *IMDB Server running in the Processes list.*

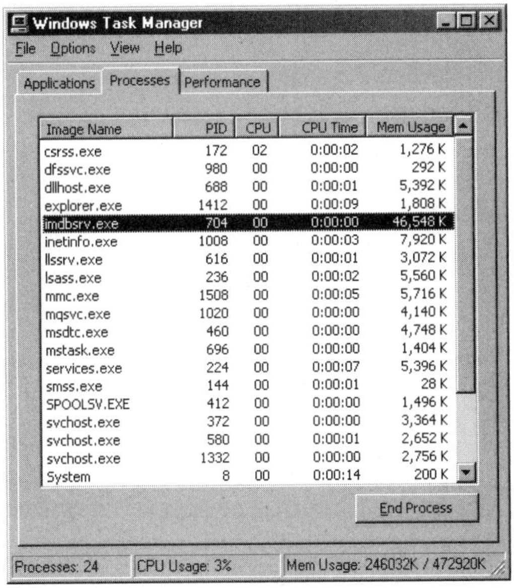

The administrator sets
up the data sources to
be cached by IMDB.

The administrator must now set up IMDB data sources, telling
IMDB which databases to front for. The property sheet for doing
this is shown in Figure 6-5. The most important piece of information here is the name of the OLE DB provider that manages the
back-end database you want to access. This example uses

Figure 6-4 *The user interface for setting the properties of IMDB Server.*

Figure 6-5 *The user interface for configuring IMDB data sources.*

MSDASQL, an OLE DB layer that provides access to Microsoft SQL Server. The Provider Properties are a connection string passed to the database provider, which in this case contain the user ID and password for verification.

Once you have the data source configured, you must specify which tables within the data source you want IMDB to cache. Use the Component Services snap-in to create a new table, and then enter its name. The only property that a table provides is whether or not to enable the replication of BLOBs from the table. Normally, only typed data is replicated from the database to the IMDB cache. However, if you enable loading of BLOBs as shown in Figure 6-6, any BLOB in the database that is smaller than the cache BLOB size will also be replicated.

The administrator then specifies the tables within each source to be cached.

That's all you have to do to configure IMDB. To run the sample, set up the sample ASP pages as directed in the instructions, then open the page IMDBSAMPLEA.ASP in Internet Explorer. This is a simple ASP form page where the user can specify the parameters

The sample client accesses IMDB through an ASP page.

Figure 6-6 *Determining whether BLOBs are replicated to the IMDB cache.*

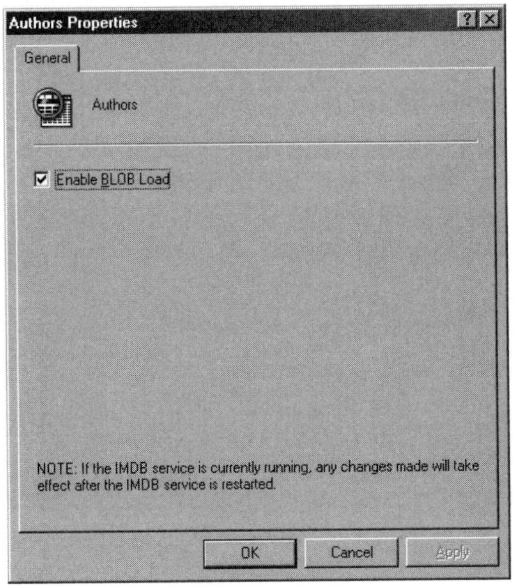

for searching through the database. You must open this page with a fully qualified URL—for example, *http://mycomputer/ IMDBSamp1A.asp*—for the ASP script to compile correctly. You will then see the page shown in Figure 6-7. You have to select the Display Data check box if you want to view the ADO Recordset that is returned to the client from IMDB; otherwise, the only information you will see is the amount of time it took to retrieve the Recordset.

The ASP script uses ADO to access IMDB.

When the user clicks the Submit button, these parameters are passed to another ASP page called *IMDBSamp1B*, which is where the work gets done. The VBScript on this page is never viewed directly by the user; it is instead executed as part of the process of compiling the ASP page. A listing of the relevant code portion is shown in Figure 6-8. The script uses ADO to open a connection to

Figure 6-7 *The IMDB sample application.*

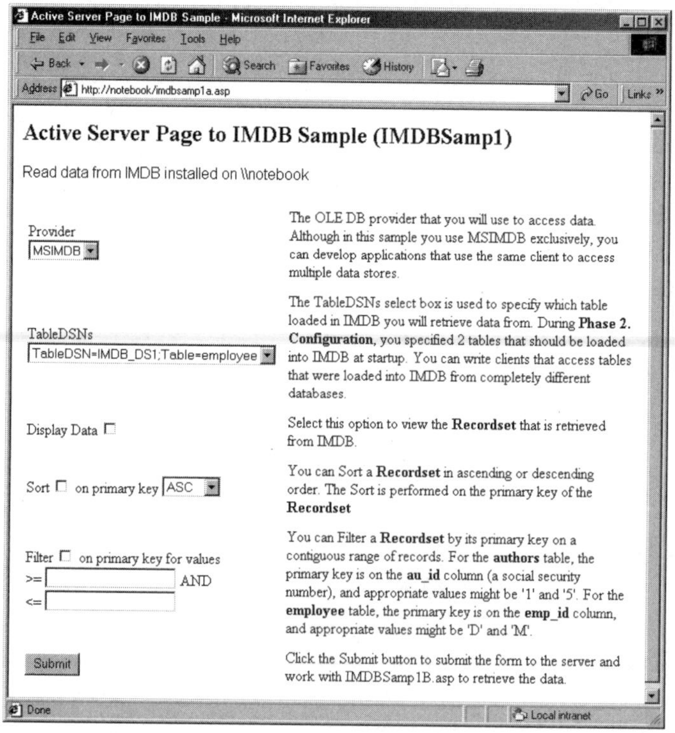

the tables that the administrator set up to be provided by IMDB. This is exactly what you would do when accessing any other database. The only difference is the provider name that you put in—MSIMDB. For more information on programming ADO, consult "ADO: Learn to Love It" by Rob Macdonald in the April 1998 issue of *Visual Basic Developer*, available on the MSDN CD-ROM .

Figure 6-8 *Using ADO in IMDBSAMP1B.ASP to open a connection to the IMDB data cache.*

```
Dim cn
Set cn = Server.CreateObject ("ADODB.Connection")

cn.Provider = "MSIMDB"
cn.ConnectionString = "IMDB_DS1"
cn.CursorLocation = 1 ' adUseNone
cn.Open
```

When the connection takes place, the IMDB Server provides the IMDB proxy object transparently, as discussed previously. The IMDB proxy routes the read request to the shared memory tables, and the results are returned in a fraction of the time required by a network hop to a database on disk. We've saved a tremendous amount of time and effort by letting go and letting COM+.

Transactional Operations with IMDB

All operations in IMDB use COM+ transactions to protect the integrity of the database system. When accessed by a COM+ object that already belongs to a transaction, IMDB enlists in the transaction transparently and does what you think it ought to do. (Read Chapter 3 if you're not sure what it ought to do.) The developer of the IMDB client doesn't have to think about it, just as the developer of an object that used SQL server in a transaction didn't have to.

IMDB operations use COM+ transactions to protect database integrity.

MTS and the concept of combining resource managers from different sources into a single transaction didn't really exist at the time OLE DB was developed. Accordingly, an OLE DB provider generally exposes a number of standard OLE DB interfaces that

IMDB does not use OLE DB's internal transaction mechanism.

IMDB gets all of its
transaction services
from the COM+ DTC.

allow its clients to perform their own transacted operations within that OLE DB provider—for example, making certain that updates to two tables in the same provider either succeed or fail atomically together. Because it lives in the COM+ run-time environment, which provides much broader protection, IMDB does not support any of these OLE DB transaction interfaces. IMDB clients that attempt to use them directly, perhaps because of using legacy code, will fail. IMDB gets all of its transaction services from the COM+ DTC.

You might remember from the discussion of transactions in Chapter 3 that in SQL Server it was up to each database administrator to specify the locking and isolation levels that applied to each table. Some are better in high-contention cases, some in low-contention. It is the administrator's job to choose, based on the type of data and what the clients are going to be doing with it. IMDB requires you to specify the levels programmatically, using code similar to that shown in the sample program.

The isolation model specifies how a transaction's data is visible to another transaction. The following problems can occur:

- *Nonrepeatable read* Transaction A reads a row. Transaction B updates or deletes that row and commits this change. If transaction A attempts to reread the row, it will receive different row values or discover that the row has been deleted.

- *Phantom* Transaction A reads a set of rows that satisfy some search criteria. Transaction B inserts a row that matches the search criteria. If transaction A reexecutes the statement that read the rows, it receives a different set of rows, including an inserted "phantom."

The default isolation level for IMDB is called *Read Committed*. A client reading data at this level can see changes made by any committed transaction at any time (although not one still in progress, one that has not committed). No locks are used. This level of isolation is quite fast, but nonrepeatable reads and phantoms are both possible. This shouldn't bother most applications in the read-often, write-seldom model that IMDB was designed to support.

The next slower, but safer, level of isolation is called *Repeatable Read*. A transaction operating at this level is guaranteed to not see any changes made by other transactions in values it has already read. A nonrepeatable read is not possible here, but a phantom is.

The slowest but safest choice is called *Serializable*. Operating at this level guarantees that all concurrent transactions will interact only in ways that produce the same effect as if each transaction were entirely executed one after the other. Neither nonrepeatable reads nor phantoms are possible at this isolation level.

The latter two isolation levels use locks to provide the specified isolation; these locks can be of the optimistic or pessimistic type. Optimistic locking, the default, doesn't actually block other users from accessing the data; it just aborts the read if any of them actually do. Because it doesn't actually acquire a lock when it accesses the data, it is faster to execute but slower to recover when an error actually happens. It's like an intersection without a traffic light, but with a wrecker standing by. You use it when you think contention is rare, which is most of the time in the read-often, write-seldom model that IMDB was designed to optimize. Pessimistic locking acquires a lock before every access to data. It therefore runs much more slowly than optimistic locking, but you won't get any aborts for violating isolation. It's like an intersection with a demand-regulated traffic light. You use this when contention is likely.

In its default isolation level (*Read Committed*) and during read operations, the IMDB proxy DLL does not take any locks on the shared memory file. This default can provide huge performance gains to middle-tier components that are doing lots of reads from IMDB. COM+ component developers building middle-tier

> The *Read Committed, Repeatable Read*, and *Serializable* transaction isolation levels are implemented for IMDB.

> IMDB features either optimistic or pessimistic locking.

application servers are advised to keep read-oriented data on IMDB and use the *Read Committed* isolation level.

Security in IMDB

Security is fundamental to the operation of any database scheme, and IMDB is no exception. To obtain optimum speed from IMDB, it is necessary to think about security in advance.

Only members of the IMDB Trusted User role can access IMDB.

COM+ automatically restricts the use of IMDB to groups of users designated by the administrator. The COM+ system application contains a role called *IMDB Trusted User*, as shown in Figure 6-9. Only members of this role are allowed to access IMDB. If non-members try, they get an error. You must assign to this role the accounts of the security principals under whose identity you will run your middle-tier IMDB clients. You may find it easiest to create a Windows 2000 security group called Trusted IMDB Users, assign this group to that role, and add new security principals to the group as they come in. The IMDB clients themselves must provide any access control required by their business logic. This is the *trusted-server* security model described in Chapter 2.

Figure 6-9 *The IMDB Trusted User role.*

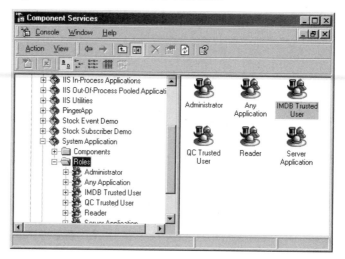

The next question is the security relationship between IMDB and its underlying OLE DB provider. The administrator sets the user identity under which the IMDB Server runs, currently by using the administration tools for services. The default is to use the LocalSystem account, and the IMDB Server will read its underlying databases as this user. When the default LocalSystem account is used, the IMDB Server cannot access remote databases. To access remote databases, the administrator should configure the IMDB Server to run as a specific user identity and give that user read access to all the tables that the administrator wants IMDB to cache and to the schemas for these tables.

When an IMDB client writes to IMDB, the proxy routes the write to the IMDB Server, and the server passes it through to the underlying database. Writing to databases generally requires some amount of security checking. In IMDB, the Server has a choice of the trusted-server model or the impersonation/delegation model. The advantages and disadvantages of these choices were discussed in Chapter 2. The example shown in this chapter uses the trusted-server approach. The impersonation/delegation model appears in IMDB documentation, but no examples are available at the time of this writing.

> The IMDB Server has a choice of the trusted-server or impersonation/ delegation security models.

IMDB Design Considerations

As with transactions and Queued Components, IMDB was developed to solve a specific type of problem. IMDB has its own worldview, its own gestalt, its own religious philosophy, its own dietary laws. It's not hard to worship at IMDB's shrine: just set it up administratively as shown, and programming is a snap. But as with other parts of COM+, IMDB requires careful thought at design time to plan your application in a manner that makes best use of the features of IMDB while avoiding its drawbacks.

> Using IMDB requires paying careful attention to design.

The most frequently read database tables should reside in IMDB.

Reading data in IMDB is blisteringly fast compared to fetching the same data from a persistent database on another machine. The most important thing you can do is to get your most frequently read data off the iron and into silicon via IMDB. Use whatever SQL views or database administration tricks you need to cajole frequently read information into a table that IMDB can cache in RAM on the middle-tier machine.

The limitations of available RAM require careful choices about the data to cache.

The RAM cache on an IMDB server is often much smaller than the underlying database. Even though it has become less expensive than it was, RAM still costs about 100 times as much as the same amount of space on an iron disk. Even if we could afford it, current versions of the operating system are limited to less than 3 GB of RAM on an Intel machine, and 28 GB on an Alpha, as described later in the "Using IMDB with the Very Large Memory Model" section of this chapter. This sounds like a lot of RAM, but its value depends on what you are storing. That amount of space will indeed hold a large number of still photographs from the Victoria's Secret catalog; it will hold many fewer minutes of their high-resolution fashion-show videos. Depending on the amount of data you have, you will have to make choices about exactly which pieces of data you want to cache in IMDB.

IMDB operates only on a whole-table basis. If you don't have enough RAM to cache your entire database, consider separating its entries in a way that matches the frequency of access. For example, a bookstore that doesn't have enough memory to store its entire catalog in IMDB might split its inventory into two tables, one for bestsellers and one for other books. The bookstore might place the bestseller table in IMDB because of its frequent access. The table could be set as a database view and generated weekly to track sales.

IMDB is unable to cache anything smaller than a whole database table.

IMDB doesn't support *vertical partitioning*, by which I mean caching only some of the columns of the tables it reads. To conserve space, make certain that the database tables you cache in IMDB contain only the columns you really need. The bookstore would probably design its IMDB table to contain author, title, and a short synopsis, but it would store the columns holding weekly sales statistics for the last 100 weeks in a different table so as not to waste IMDB cache space on this less frequently used data.

IMDB reads metadata from the back-end database tables and recreates in IMDB the same indexes that the database had on its back-end server machine. So be sure to optimize indexes defined on back-end database tables prior to using them with IMDB. Users must know that a specific table is present and must know the available indexes for that table. IMDB does not currently permit its clients to enumerate the available tables.

IMDB caching is not restricted to databases that are backed by a persistent store. IMDB clients can create tables in RAM for storing transient data. While not as fast as reading, writing to a table cached in shared memory is much faster than writing to an iron disk on another machine. IMDB clients can use caching to share state, for example, within a transaction.

IMDB can create new tables in RAM for storing transient data.

You can access IMDB either through ADO or at a lower level through OLE DB. The latter is significantly faster; the former significantly easier to program. Most companies will at least prototype in ADO because its higher level of abstraction makes development much easier and faster. The developer can then profile an operation to see whether any bottlenecks that exist are in the business logic or in the database access code. If the culprit is the data access code, you can rewrite it to use OLE DB.

Clients can access IMDB either through ADO or OLE DB.

IMDB is not currently able to subscribe to updates in the underlying database tables. If programs make changes to these tables other than through IMDB, IMDB won't know about them, which means the clients won't see them either. Changes to the underlying database need to be made either through IMDB or while IMDB is not running.

IMDB does not see changes in the underlying database other than those made through it.

Specifics of the OLE DB Implementation of IMDB

IMDB's implementation of OLE DB is special.

Because of the special nature of the IMDB OLE DB provider, some of the interfaces and functions differ from the standard OLE DB definition. As previously stated, IMDB does not support any of the OLE DB transaction interfaces; IMDB receives its transaction services from COM+ instead. IMDB also does not support OLE DB notifications: there is currently no way for an IMDB client to be informed when an item changes its value.

IMDB doesn't currently support a SQL-based command interface. The execution of standard SQL queries against the IMDB cache is not possible. IMDB instead exposes its data through the *IOpenRowset* application interface, which enables the IMDB clients to actually browse the cached tables and use defined indexes to sort and filter the data. The IMDB approach makes it very efficient and inexpensive to create *HROWS* and access the same data in multiple concurrent processes.

The only bindings that are supported by IMDB are by-value or by-reference into client-owned memory. It is not possible to create an accessor that binds to memory owned by IMDB or to reference accessors. (An OLE DB accessor is a collection of information that describes not only how data is stored in a database buffer but how the database must transfer the data.)

IMDB accepts only two of ADO's connection string arguments: *Provider* and *Data Source*. Any other arguments that you specify for this property will return error 3251.

Using IMDB with the Very Large Memory Model

I thought we'd never use up a 4-GB address space.

I remember attending the Windows NT prerelease conference in San Francisco in 1992, at which Microsoft first revealed the details of their flat 32-bit memory model. My fellow geeks and I toasted the demise of near and far pointers with some excellent beer and told each other that we'd be long dead before anyone used up that amount of address space on a PC. We still had a desktop mindset at that time.

Now that we are using main memory for storing databases, the availability of RAM becomes critical. Enterprise databases can easily be 100 GB or more, and once you start storing images or sound (not to mention video), memory requirements can go through the ceiling, and your 4-GB address space can look pretty puny. The standard Win32 memory model provides 4 GB of address space per process, of which 2 GB are reserved for the operating system and 2 GB are available to the programmer. A COM+ application can tell Windows 2000 to allow 3 GB for the program and only 1 GB for the operating system. To do this, you check the Enable 3GB Support check box on the Advanced tab of the application's property sheet as shown in Figure 6-10. It's not a lot, but it's something.

It took about five years.

Figure 6-10 *Enabling 3-GB support on the Advanced tab of the application's property sheet.*

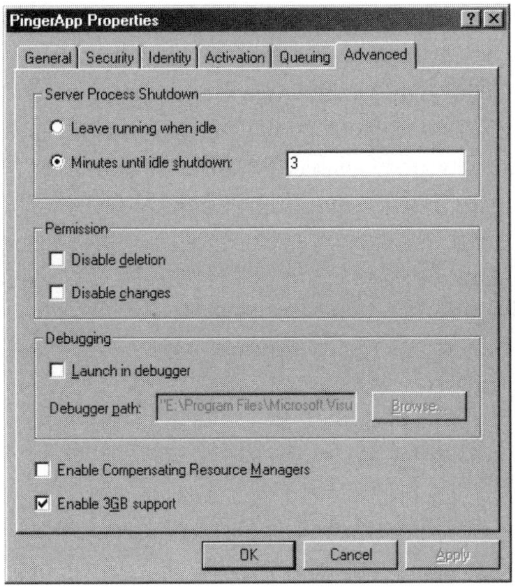

You can expand memory beyond the 4-GB boundary and into the 64-bit address space on a Compaq Alpha APX system running Windows 2000. This allows access to up to 32 GB of memory. This memory extension is called Very Large Memory (VLM) and contains a 64-bit pointer data type (*_ptr64* in Visual C++ for the Alpha) with a corresponding Win32 memory management API. Now we're back to the bad old days of two kinds of pointers. What should we call them today, far and humongously far pointers?

As an alternative to a special memory management API, IMDB provides transparent access to as much main memory as is physically available, as shown in Figure 6-11, because IMDB already uses VLM. You can now use IMDB for large arrays, for example, instead of having to code all the VLM yourself.

A full solution to the 32-bit main memory address-range performance bottleneck, of course, is the upcoming 64-bit architectures for Windows. Using IMDB today means that you won't have to rewrite the data access portions of your application to run on larger machines when 64-bit systems and processors become available. Furthermore, by treating the extended address space as an IMDB, application developers have a high-level means of cached database access through every programming language capable of dealing with COM objects. Even when true 64-bit Windows development tools are available, IMDB will stand as a valid software design technique for improving performance at a higher development level.

Figure 6-11 *Using IMBD to access Very Large Memory.*

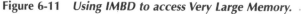

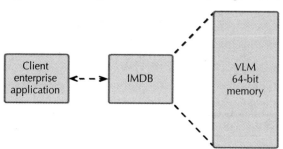

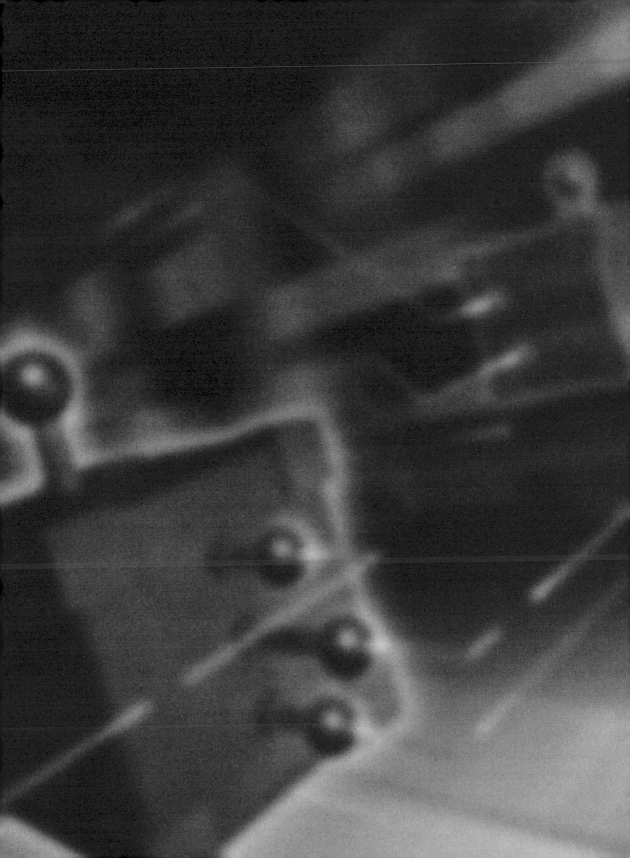

Chapter Seven

Load Balancing

Load-Balancing Problem Background

Enterprise applications have to worry about the ratio of clients to server resources in a way that desktop applications never did. COM desktop application servers typically have one or two clients, occasionally three or four, but not hundreds. In an enterprise application, however, when a COM server accepts incoming object creation requests and method calls from network clients, the number of clients per server can jump dramatically. This increased demand requires design-time attention to maintain acceptable levels of performance for the clients. A server box on a network will start its first day with a few clients. As word gets around of the services available from the server (stock trades, song clips, Microsoft jokes), more and more clients will start using it and its performance will drop below acceptable levels. You can add more RAM or CPU chips to the server, but at a certain point, the box won't stretch anymore and you'll need to buy a second box to work side by side with the first one. This is easy enough and not usually too expensive. However, just plugging in the box won't solve the problem: you somehow have to divide the users among the two servers.

Enterprise applications often need to balance their client loads over more than one server.

From the developer point of view, the easiest way to do this would appear to be simply telling half the clients to use server A and the other half to use server B—static load balancing. However,

Static load balancing is difficult and expensive to administer correctly.

this classic approach has a number of problems. First, the administrative work of pointing each client at the right server is expensive and hard to implement correctly. Suppose you have 100 clients on one server, it's too slow, so you buy another. You probably want to even the clients out, with 50 using each server. Now you have to tell 50 users about the new server you want them to use, and they have to go to their UI and enter the name of the new server in an options dialog. What happens if they don't get around to it? What happens if they do it incorrectly? What happens if the wrong users do it? Not only does the process cost you time and money, it costs the users time and money, and you have no control over when, how, or even whether the assignment of clients to the new server gets implemented. And when you are up to 200 subscribers and need to add a third server, you have to do it all over again. What would you want to do to a phone company who made you change area codes twice in a year? We'd really like our load-balancing algorithm to be deterministic and easy to use for clients and servers. The static approach is neither.

With static load balancing, the assignment of clients to servers doesn't vary as the client load varies.

The second problem of static load balancing is that the assignment of clients to servers does not vary as the client load varies. Suppose a blizzard in one state causes school to be canceled, and all the homebound kids want to juggle their stock portfolios after watching *Sesame Street*. If you've assigned clients to the server closest to their geographical location, one server will be heavily loaded while the other becomes an expensive paperweight. The same thing happens with international time zones. Australian and Japanese users are most active when U.S. users on the East Coast are winding down. The static load-balancing algorithm cannot track even coarse-grained variations of user load. The wasted server sits around, spinning its disks, while users on the heavily loaded servers fume. Think how you feel when you see a bank clerk filing her nails while you wait in line for the one teller who's actually working. We'd really like our load-balancing mechanism to respond to the *actual*, rather than a hypothetical, load on the system at any given time. The static approach doesn't do this.

The third problem of static load balancing is that it doesn't easily handle a downed server. Splitting the server resources among several boxes is supposed to afford the system some degree of continuity and robustness: if you have four boxes and one goes down, you'd really like the other three to pick up the load as best they can. But this doesn't work with static load balancing. All the clients that are pointed at the malfunctioning server are disabled themselves. You could give them each a backup server name to try, as many online services do with dial-up numbers, but the same administrative problems described previously will come back to bite you. The last thing you want is your client having to worry about the location of its server. We'd really like our load-balancing mechanism to dynamically track the available hardware, assigning incoming clients to all the available server boxes while bypassing those that are nonfunctional.

Static load balancing is not responsive to changing conditions.

Solution Architecture

To avoid the problems outlined in the previous section, we need a load-balancing mechanism that is dynamic rather than static, one that will detect the available servers and the current load on each and then apportion clients to the least busy server. Furthermore, we need all of this work done without excessive difficulty to the administrator setting it up or to the developer designing products that use it. Finally, we need the load-balancing operation itself to be efficient—spending five minutes figuring out which server machine to use for a ten-second operation would be no savings.

Modern enterprise applications require automatic dynamic load balancing.

You could certainly sit down and write such a load-balancing system. All of your client applications would first connect to a master machine called, say, the router. The router would then direct the client to the least busy server available at the time. The servers would have some type of mechanism for continually indicating their presence and their current load to the router so that the router could properly direct the incoming clients. It's not conceptually difficult; a few good geeks could probably get it done in a year—that is, if you had a few extra geeks and a spare year. We'd really rather inherit a load balancer from the operating system than write our own. Have you finally seen the pattern in this book?

COM+ provides a dynamic load-balancing service that automatically distributes the creation of COM objects over multiple server machines.

COM+ provides the Component Load Balancing (CLB) service , a dynamic load-balancing service that does all of these things for distributing the creation of COM objects as evenly as possible over multiple server machines. The layout of the system is shown in Figure 7-1.

Figure 7-1   *Load-balancing network configuration.*

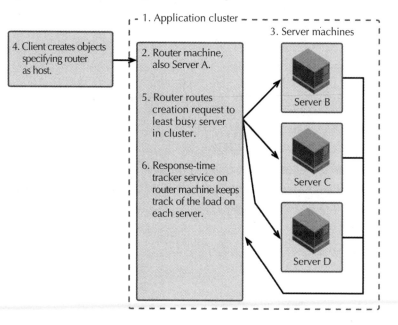

COM+'s load balancing designates one server as the router, which distributes object creation requests to all servers in a cluster.

The administrator sets up a *CLB cluster,* also known as an *application cluster* (1), which is the set of server machines available for spreading out the load. The administrator does this by first designating a server machine to act as the router (2), formally known as the Application Cluster Router or sometimes the CLB Server (just what we need, another overloaded meaning for the term "server"). The administrator then uses the Component Services snap-in to add server machines (3) to the cluster. At the time of this writing, the router requires either Windows 2000 Advanced Server or Windows 2000 Data Center, but the nonrouter server machines can run Windows 2000 Server. The client applications create their COM objects as usual, specifying the router as the host (4). When the router receives an incoming request to create an object, it checks which server in the cluster, including itself, is the least busy. The router sends the creation request to the selected server or handles it itself, and the creation request actually happens on this server (5). The client then talks directly to the object on the selected server machine. The router runs a response-time tracker service (6) that the servers keep updated so that the router knows which ones are busiest.

Simplest Load-Balancing Example

The simplest example of a load-balancing server is the Load Balancing sample application available on this book's Web site. It contains an extremely simple component with a single method called *GetMachineName*, which calls the *GetComputerName* function to retrieve the name of the machine on which it is running. The client creates an object, calls this method, and sees which machine its object is actually on.

A load-balancing example begins here.

You will find that using the load-balancing service is primarily an administrative exercise. Developers don't need to do much to use it, nor can they do much to alter its behavior in this release of the operating system. These design considerations are described later in this chapter in the sections on load-balanced component and load-balanced client design, but as you will see, there aren't many to think about.

COM+ load balancing is primarily an administrative task.

The first thing to do in this sample is to set up the application cluster using the Component Services snap-in. The user interface is shown in Figure 7-2.

Figure 7-2   *Setting up the application cluster.*

You must check the box that says Use This Computer As The Load Balancing Server, as shown, to designate the specified machine as the router of its cluster. The operating system will launch its load-balancing service on the router machine the next time it starts up. Next you have to add machines to the Application Cluster box, as shown in the figure. The router machine will route requests for all applications it contains to all the server machines in the cluster. This is the only option supported in the current release of the operating system. The router cannot balance application A between servers 1 and 2 and application B between servers 2 and 3.

Now you need to create a new COM+ application on the router machine and install the component from the Load Balancing sample into it. This process should be pretty standard by now. You then need to mark the component as supporting dynamic load

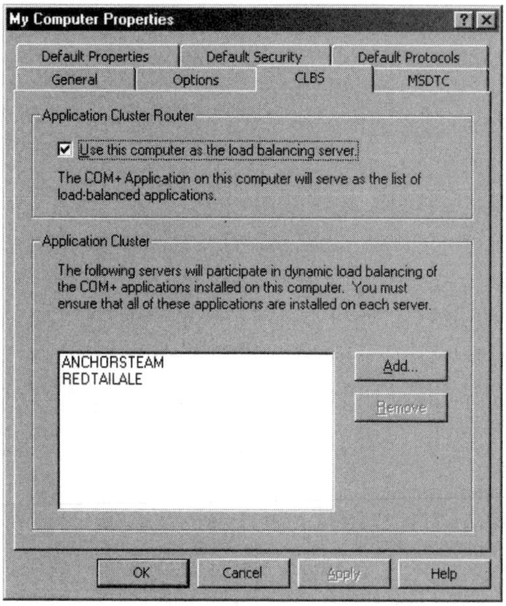

The administrator designates one server machine as the router for an application cluster and assigns other server machines to the cluster.

balancing, using the Component Services snap-in as shown in Figure 7-3. You must install the application containing the component on every machine in the application cluster.

This tells COM+ that the component has been written in such a manner so as to not care which machine its objects are created on, as described later in the "Load-Balancing Component Design" section of this chapter.

The administrator must specify which components can be load balanced.

Now you need to distribute the application and the component to all the relevant server machines. Use the Component Services snap-in to export the application. The server machines in your cluster must then import it using their own Component Services snap-ins.

The administrator must install the load-balanced COM+ application on all server machines in the cluster.

That's really all you need to do. Now run the sample base client application, shown in Figure 7-4.

Figure 7-3 *The user interface for load balancing.*

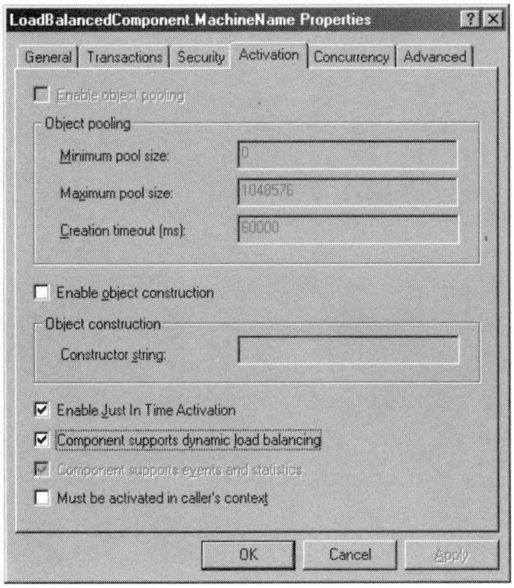

Figure 7-4   *The Load Balancing sample client application.*

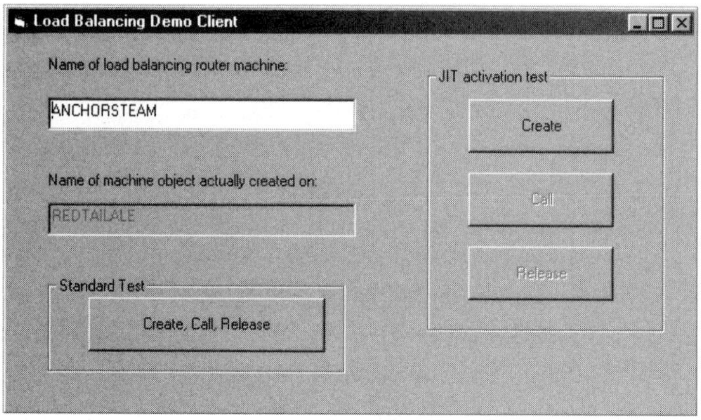

Instructions for running
the Load Balancing
sample client applica-
tion appear here.

Type the name of the load-balancing router into the top text control and click the Create, Call, Release button in the Standard Test
group box. This causes the client application to request that an
object be created on the load-balancing router machine. The
router picks the least busy machine from its application cluster
and bounces the creation request over to it. The object is actually
created on the latter machine. When the client application calls
GetMachineName, the component responds with the name of the
machine on which it is actually running, which will appear in the
lower edit box control. Do this a few times, and you'll see the
server name change as the router apportions the creation requests
among the available servers in the cluster.

COM+ performs load balancing only when an object is initially
created. If the object supports just-in-time activation (see Chapter 3), subsequent JIT activations of a specific object instance are
always performed on the server on which the object was first created. Remember how JIT activation works—when the object is
deactivated, the actual object is destroyed on the server, but the
client-side proxy, the server-side stub, and the channel connecting
them stay in place. The connection between the client and the
specific machine (the plumbing) is not destroyed, even though the
actual server-side component (the faucet) is. You can demonstrate

this feature with the sample by configuring the Load Balancing sample component to use JIT activation. You will have to set the component for Auto-Done as well, because the component does not set the deactivate-on-return bit on its own. Clicking the Create button creates the object, invoking COM+ load balancing. Clicking the Call button calls the component's *GetMachineName* method. Each time you do this, the object is activated (a new instance is created) just in time. You will see that the location of the component doesn't change when you repeatedly click the Call button. Clicking the Release button causes the client to release the component, destroying not only the actual object, but also the proxy, stub, and channel. If you click the Create button again, the creation operation will invoke the load-balancing mechanism again.

Load-Balanced Component Design

When designing a component that can support load balancing it is essential that you avoid any sort of location dependency, since the component can never know ahead of time which machine it will be running on. For example, you can't depend on the location of specific files, such as C:\MYDIRECTORY\SOMEFILE, unless you are positive that every server machine will have the same file in the same location.

Location dependencies can be subtle. If an object on server A enters a foreign exchange deal into a database at 0900 hours and an object on server B enters a local deal at 0901 hours, which one actually happens first? It depends on the time zones the two servers are using. If the servers are or might someday be in different physical locations, you probably want to write your component to use a single time standard for all of its work, regardless of the time zone setting of the machine on which it finds itself running. Barclays Bank, headquartered in London, will probably run all of its servers on Greenwich Mean Time, regardless of their physical location, whereas the LL Bean mail-order servers will probably run on the Eastern Time used in Freeport, Maine.

Designers of load-balanced components must carefully avoid any sort of location dependency.

Since you don't know on which machine a component's objects will next be created, you must be very careful about state management when designing load-balanceable components. For example, the object may receive its initial state from parameters passed by the client, or it may retrieve its initial state from a database outside the machine on which it runs. Objects can retrieve a machine-dependent state, such as the DSN for a specific machine, by using object constructor strings. For more discussion on the location of state in COM+, see Chapter 3.

Load-Balanced Client Design

A client application doesn't do anything different when creating a component that is load-balanced than it does when creating one that isn't. The client application simply creates an object, specifying the load-balancing router as the host. The client doesn't know whether the object that resulted from the call is running on the machine it specified or on one to which the router delegated the object creation. In general, you probably don't want your clients to have to care whether their components are load balanced or not.

A client should be aware that if a component is load balanced, a server dying doesn't necessarily mean that the client is useless until that server comes back up. The application cluster may contain other servers that can take over the load. Suppose a client creates an object that, after load balancing, actually resides on server A. The client makes a few calls on the object, then server A blows its power supply and dies. In this case, the next time the client makes a call on the object, the call will time out, and the client will receive an error code indicating that the server has in fact died. The client should, at this point, release its object and try to re-create it; the router will route the creation request to a server that is still running. A client that thinks it might be using a load-balanced component should release and re-create the object when it encounters a server failure.

Handling Router Failure

You've probably figured out by now that one potential weak spot in COM+'s load-balancing system is the router. Since all load-balancing object requests initially come into the router, if that machine blows its power supply and dies we have lots of angry clients and up to seven other servers functioning as room heaters. That's bad, especially when you've used the load-balancing capability to build up your customer's expectations. Imagine if the Super Bowl telecast got taken down by one plug falling out of the wall.

Any reliability engineer will tell you that although you can gold-plate systems until your head falls off, something you didn't think of, something you forgot to guard against, will kill you. Lifesaving reliability comes not from gold-plating, but from having backup systems, and backups on the backups. While COM+ only supports one load-balancing router at a time, you can use Microsoft Clustering Services, formerly known as Wolfpack, to configure another server in the cluster to take over the router's function in the event the router goes down. A discussion of this mechanism is beyond the scope of this book. In quick conceptual terms, the spare router keeps track of a heartbeat sent by the primary router. When the heartbeat fails, the spare takes over the network name of the primary, so that network requests directed to the primary will arrive at the spare. In this way, COM+ load balancing avoids having a single point of failure.

You can set up Microsoft Clustering Services (Wolfpack) to provide a hot spare for the router, thus avoiding a single point of failure.

Future Directions

Windows 2000 represents the first release of COM+ load balancing. In order to get it out on schedule, this release won't contain several requested features, which may or may not appear in future versions. I present them here only for the purpose of discussion. The first of these features is pluggable load-balancing algorithms. In the current version, you don't have a choice as to how the load-balancing system decides what the load is on any given server. It always uses the generic response-time tracker that comes as part of the operating system. That's a very reasonable first cut, but you might want to write a load-balancing algorithm that more closely tracks your underlying business processes. For example, for legal or political reasons, you might want to assign incoming clients to the least busy server that's physically in (or *not* physically in, depending on what you're doing) the country of the client. I hope this feature appears in future releases.

Another feature discussed among power-hungry geeks is load balancing the load balancer. The system currently supports only one router per cluster. When this router gets overloaded, the whole system slows down. Although a single router fits reasonably well with the current scale of the system (up to eight servers per application cluster), as the cluster size increases the need for more than one router may emerge.

Finally, I'd like to see load balancing occur at JIT activation time rather than only at creation time. If a client creates an object that uses JIT activation and then hangs on to the object for a week while performing many JIT operations on it, the object gets created and destroyed many times, all of which occur on the system on which it was first created. Server loads will most closely approach equality if the lifetimes of the objects are short.

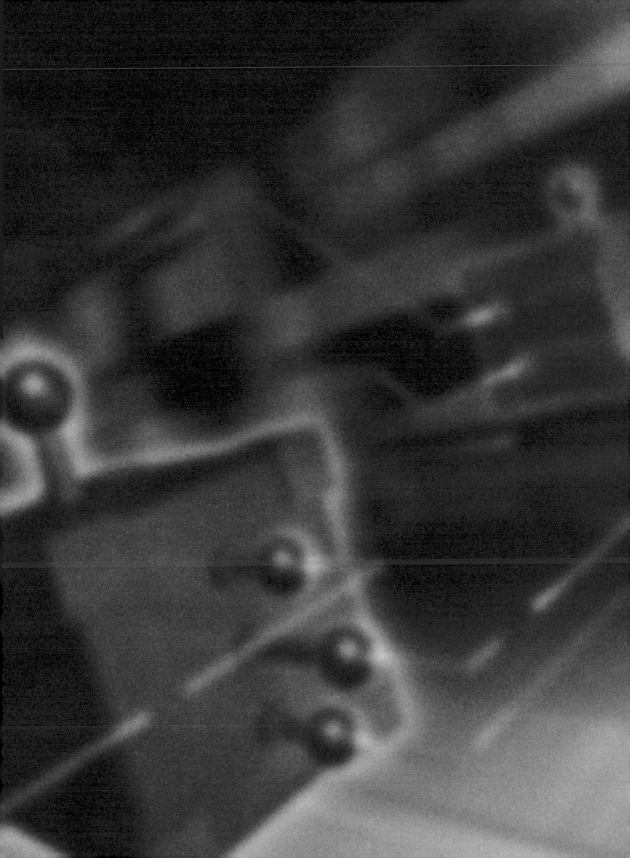

Epilogue

As you've seen throughout this book, COM+ provides the prefabricated infrastructure that you need to develop enterprise applications. Without it, you would spend so much time developing this infrastructure that you would never get to develop your business logic. With it, you can actually develop your business logic in a reasonable timeframe for a reasonable cost, and actually ship an enterprise application that does useful work for its purchaser and makes you money.

I once had an engineering professor who would say, "Engineering is doing for fifty cents what any damn fool can do for five bucks." He would have loved COM+. I was privileged to study under this man, the late Fred Hooven, while I attended the Thayer School of Engineering at Dartmouth. Listening to him spin a yarn was as close as I'm likely to get to sitting at the feet of Robert Heinlein's character Lazarus Long, the galaxy's oldest human. Hooven conducted aerodynamic experiments with Orville Wright while Wright was headmaster of the school Hooven attended. He developed a radio direction finder that might have saved Amelia Earhart if she hadn't balked at the price. He won a paper airplane contest held by *Scientific American*, and on and on. At first I had trouble believing anyone could have actually done everything that he said he had, but every story of his that I took the trouble to verify turned out to be an understatement.

Hooven spent most of his career at the Ford Motor Company, helping to build one of the modern industrial giants that have sculpted society into its current form. Looking back near the end of a very full life, he felt that his greatest accomplishment was that he and the fellow engineers of his generation "put a nation on wheels." The results of that achievement, good and bad, permeate our society to such a degree that we usually don't think about them; it's just the way things are.

I thought then that the world had changed, that it no longer held the challenges for my generation that it had held for earlier ones. There was no longer any Wild West to tame, no Industrial Revolution to build, no fascist dragons to slay. All that my generation could look forward to was holding endless committee meetings, squabbling about how to divide the pie baked by previous ones. I don't think that anymore. Sculpting the information society—bringing about what Frances Cairncross called "the death of distance" in her landmark book of that title—is an eminently worthy challenge for this generation or any other. You and I, my fellow geeks, in our twilight, will spin yarns for our somewhat skeptical grandchildren about how we connected a planet.

As doctor and poet William Carlos Williams wrote in 1917 in his poem "Tract":

>   *... Share with us*
> *share with us—it will be money*
> *in your pockets.*
>   *Go now*
> *I think you are ready.*

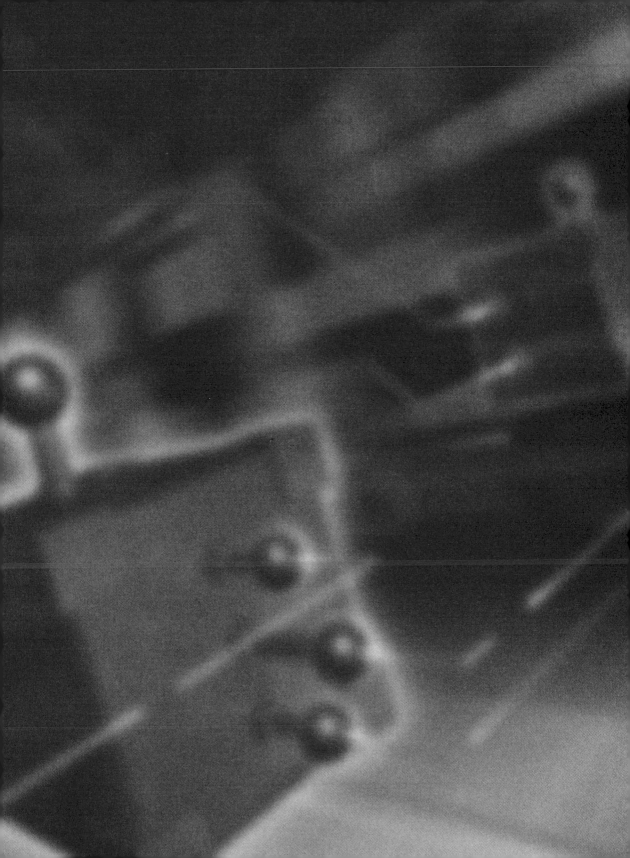

Index

B

Bank sample application, 72–83
base clients
  and authorization roles, 48, 49
  and database security, 56–57
  defined, 73, *74*
  and IMDB, 187–88
  in QC Shipping sample application, 125,
    125, 126
BeginAbort method, 111, *111*
BeginCommit method, 111, *111*
BeginPrepare method, 110, *111*
bill-paying applications
  business logic background, 69–71
  sample user interface, 73, *73*
  transaction workflow example, 72–83
binary large objects (BLOBs), 191, *192*, 193,
  193
  Cache BLOB Size setting, 191, *192*, 193
binding, defined, 144
BLOBs. *See* binary large objects (BLOBs)
business logic vs. infrastructure, 17, 18, 19–20,
  69–71
business rules, 180–81

C

C++ language, 13
caching, IMDB, 200, 201
callback process, 133–36
Callers property, *52*
calls, nested, 66
CanBePooled method, *102,* 104
catalogs. *See* COM+ catalog
causality IDs, 66
classes vs. components, 32, 33. *See also*
  event classes
class factories, defined, 144
CLB clusters, 210–11, *210*, 211–12, *212*
CLB Server, 210

clients. *See also* base clients
  and COM+ interception process, 20–23
  sharing objects, 67
  specifying authentication level, 45–47, *47*
  storing object states, 99, *99*
CoGetObjectContext function, 42, 92
CoGetObject function, 125, 143
CoImpersonateClient function, 56
CoInitializeEx function, 58–59
CoInitializeSecurity function, 45
collections, 38–39
COM+
  vs. classic COM, 6–9, 20–22
  creating object context, 40–43
  Event service, 8, 154–57
  and In-Memory Database, 8, 187–90
  and load balancing, 8, 210–11
  overview, 6–9
  and queued components, 7–8, 118–21
  relationship to MTS, 6–7, 22, 72
  security infrastructure, 7, 44–53
  services, 7–8
  and synchronization, 8, 18, 62–67
  workflow example, 23–31
COM+ catalog
  accessing, 35
  defined, 35
  object hierarchy, 35, *37*
  persistent vs. transient subscriptions, 166, 167
  subscriptions in, 155–56, 164, 166–67
COM+ Utilities application, 127–29, *128*
COMAdminCatalogCollection component, 38,
  38
COMAdminCatalog component, 35, *36*
CommitRecord method, 111, *111*
committing transactions, 71, 80–81, *80,* 90–94,
  92, 111
communications, synchronous vs.
  asynchronous, 115–18, 142
compensating resource managers (CRMs)
  cooperating components, 107
  CRM Compensator component, 107–12

compensating resource managers (CRMs),
    continued
  CRM sample application, 107–12
  CRM Worker component, 107–12
  overview, 107
compensating transactions, 105–6
component libraries, 34
Component Load Balancing (CLB) service,
    210–11. *See also* load balancing
Component Object Model (COM) vs. COM+,
    6–9, 20–22. *See also* COM+
components
  associating with applications, 27–28
  vs. classes, 32, 33
  in compensating resource managers, 107–12
  defined, 27, 31–32
  vs. objects, 32–33
  placing in library applications, 28–29, *29*
  registering and unregistering, 33
  relationship to DLL servers, 32, 33
  and type libraries, 33–34
Component Services snap-in
  Activation Properties tab, 27–28, *28,* 101,
    102, 105, 213, *213*
  and event class installation, 158–59, *158,*
    159
  marking applications as queued, 123, *123*
  overview, 25–26, *25*
  setting server application *Identity* property,
    53, *54*
  setting synchronization support, 64–65, *65*
  specifying transaction properties, 86–87, *87*
  Subscriptions folder, 160–61, *161*
ComputerName MSMQ attribute, *146*
Connect method, *36*
consistency, as transaction property, 84–85
consistent bit. *See* transaction-vote bit
context, COM+, 40–43
context objects, 41–42, 43
context wrappers, 22, *22*
Count property, *52*
CreateInstance method, *43*
CreateObject function, 29, 73, *74*

CRM Compensator component, 107–12
CrmFilesCompensator object, 110–11, *110*
CrmFilesWorker object, 108–9, *108*
CRMs. *See* compensating resource managers
    (CRMs)
CRM Worker component, 107–12

D

databases. *See also* In-Memory Database
    (IMDB)
  access problems, 185–87
  applications as resource managers, 77
  and IMDB design considerations, 200–202
  IMDB example, 190–95
  and memory, 185–87
  security issues, 55–57, 198–99
  SQL Server as application, 76–78
  and user identity, 55–57
  Very Large Memory (VLM) model, 202–4
Deactivate method, *102,* 103, 104
deactivate-on-return bit, 91
deactivating objects, 91, 94–98, *102,* 103, *103*
DeleteFile method, 108
Delivery MSMQ attribute, *146*
Description property, *165*
desktop applications, 4, 150, 152
DirectCaller property, *52*
DisableCommit method, *43, 92,* 93
Disabled transactional attribute, 89
distributed applications. *See* enterprise
    applications
distributed transaction coordinator (DTC),
    71–83
DLL servers
  vs. .EXE servers, 33, 98
  relationship to components, 32, 33
Does Not Support Transactions attribute, 88, *90*
"done" bit. *See* deactivate-on-return bit
DtcGetTransactionManager function, 74
durability, 86
durable log file, 109, 110, 112

dynamic load balancing
   architecture, 209–11
   example, 211–15
   vs. static load balancing, 209

E

EnableCommit method, *43, 92,* 93
Enabled property, *165,* 167
EncryptAlgorithm MSMQ attribute, *147*
encryption, in authentication, 46–47
EndAbort method, 111, *111*
EndCommit method, 111, *111*
EndPrepare method, 110, *111*
enterprise applications
   basic COM+ example, 23–31
   bill-paying example, 72–83
   business logic vs. infrastructure, 17, 18,
      19–20
   vs. desktop applications, 17–18
   development challenges, 5–6
   elements of, 4
   event system example, 157–64
   example, 10–12
   In-Memory Database example, 190–95
   load-balancing example, 211–15
   overview, 4
   Pinger example, 24–31
   Publisher example, 157–64
   QC Shipping example, 122–30
   Queued Components example, 122–30
   role of COM+ in, 6–9
   Sample Bank example, 72–83
   scaling business logic, 69–71
   security services in, 7, 17, 44–53
   and server identity, 53–57
   synchronization services in, 8, 18, 62–67
   synchronous vs. asynchronous
      communications in, 115–18, 142
   transaction example, 72–83

event classes, 155, 156, *158,* 158–59, *159*
EventClassID property, *165*
event interfaces, 155, 156
event methods, 155, 156, *168*
event objects, 156, 166
events. *See also* publishers; subscribers
   background, 149–54
   COM+ Event service architecture, 8, 154–57,
      154
   combining with queued components, 176–79
   defined, 154–55
   example, 157–64
   filtering, 169–75
   firing, 155, 156, 162, *163,* 168–69, 171–75
   loosely coupled, 153
   notification architecture, 149–51, *150, 151*
   and order of receipt, 178–79
   vs. queued components, 175–76
   security issues, 181–82
   tightly coupled, 151–53, *151*
   and transactions, 179–81
.EXE vs. DLL servers, 33, 98
ExportApplication method, *36*

F

FilterCriteria property, *166*
filtering
   event calls, 169–70
   event firing process, 171–75
   subscriber parameter, 169–70
filters, publisher, 172, *173,* 174–75
FireSubscription method, *173,* 175
firing events, 155, 156, 162, *163,* 168–69,
   171–75
ForceLog method, 109, *109*
ForceTransactionToAbort method, 109, *109,*
   111
ForgetLogRecord method, *109*
FormatName MSMQ attribute, *147*

G

GetCollection method, 38, *38,* 39
GetComputerName function, 211
GetDeactivateOnReturn method, *92*
GetMachineName method, 211, 214, 215
GetMultipleComponentsInfo method, *36*
GetMyTransactionVote method, *92*
GetObjectContext function, 42, 78
GetObject function, 125, *125,* 143, 144, 145
GetSubscriptions method, 171, *172*
Get_TransactionUOW method, *109*

H

"happy" bit. *See* transaction-vote bit
HashAlgorithm MSMQ attribute, *147*

I

ICOMAdminCatalog interface, 159
IConnectionPointContainer interface, 151
IConnectionPoint interface, 151, 152
IContextState interface, 42, 92, *92,* 93
ICrmCompensator interface, 110, *111*
ICrmLogControl interface, 108–9, *109,* 110
IDispatch interface, 174
IDL. *See* Interface Definition Language (IDL)
IEventControl interface
    accessing, 171–72
    defined, 171
    methods, *172*
    in publisher filter flow, *173,* 174
IEventSubscription interface, 164, *165–66*
IFiringControl interface, *173,* 174–75
IGetContextProperties interface, 43
IIS. *See* Microsoft Internet Information Server (IIS)
IMDB. *See* In-Memory Database (IMDB)

IMDB sample application, 190–95
impersonation/delegation security model, 56–57, *56*
ImportComponent method, *36*
IMultiInterfaceEventControl interface, 174
infrastructure
    vs. business logic, 17, 18, 19–20, 69–71
    prefabricated, example of enterprise application without, 10–12
    role of, in enterprise applications, 5–9
Initialize method, *174*
In-Memory Database (IMDB)
    architecture, 187, *188*
    caching, 200, 201
    design considerations, 199–202
    example, 190–95
    list of methods, *36*
    overview, 8, 187–90
    proxy objects in, 189–90
    role of IMDB Server, 188–89, 190
    sample application, 190–95
    security issues, 198–99
    and transactions, 195–99
    Trusted User role, 198, *198*
    typical architecture, 187, *188*
    and Very Large Memory (VLM) model, 202–4
InProcServer registry entry, 59–61, *60*
in-proc servers, 32
InstallApplication method, *36*
InstallComponent method, *36*
InstallEventClass method, 159
InstallMultipleComponents method, *36*
instance variables, storing object state in, 99, *99*
interactive users, 53–54
interception, 20–23, 49, 50, *50, 51*
Interface Definition Language (IDL), 87, *87*
InterfaceID property, *166*
interfaces. *See also* user interfaces
    for Event service, 154–55, 156
    ICOMAdminCatalog, 159

S

U

undoing transactions, 105–6
user interfaces. *See also* Component Services
   snap-in
   in bill-paying sample application, 73, *73*
   in Publisher sample application, 158
users
   and role-based security, 48–52
   and server process identity, 53–57

V

VBScript, 125, *125*
Very Large Memory (VLM) model, 202–4
Visual Basic, 87, *88,* 125–26
Visual C++, 13
Visual J++, 13

W

Web site, 13
Windows 2000, 9, 14–15
Windows NT 4.0, 45
window stations, 54
wizards
   COM Component Install Wizard, 158–59,
      158, 159
   COM New Subscriptions Wizard, 160, *161*
wrappers, context, 22, *22*
WriteLogRecord method, 109, *109*
WriteLogRecordVariants method, *109*

David Platt

President and founder of Rolling Thunder
Computing, David S. Platt teaches
COM and COM+ at Harvard University
and at companies worldwide. He
is the author of three previous books,
including *The Essence of COM with
ActiveX* (Prentice Hall Computer
Books, 1998). He is the COM/ActiveX
columnist for Byte.com and is a frequent contributor to *Microsoft Systems
Journal*. Dave has a master of engineering
degree from Dartmouth College and
spends his free time scuba diving (when
he's not roller-blading). He lives in Ipswich,
Massachusetts and can be contacted at
www.rollthunder.com.

The manuscript for this book was prepared and submitted to Microsoft Press in electronic form. Text files were prepared using Microsoft Word 97. Pages were composed by Microsoft Press using Adobe PageMaker 6.52 for Windows, with text in Optima and display type in Optima Bold. Composed pages were delivered to the printer as electronic prepress files.

Cover Design
Patrick Lanfear

Cover Illustration
Todd Daman

Interior Graphic Artist
Joel Panchot

Principal Compositor
Barb Runyan

Principal Proofreader/Copy Editor
Cheryl Penner

Indexer
Julie Kawabata